AF560851

THE ATLANTIC CRITICAL STUDIES

WILLIAM SHAKESPEARE'S

The Merchant of Venice

THE ATLANTIC CRITICAL STUDIES

WILLIAM SHAKESPEARE'S
The Merchant of Venice

RATRI RAY

Published by

ATLANTIC®

PUBLISHERS & DISTRIBUTORS
B-2, Vishal Enclave, Opp. Rajouri Garden,
New Delhi-110027
Phones : 25413460, 25429987, 25466842
Sales Office
7/22, Ansari Road, Darya Ganj,
New Delhi-110002
Phones : 23273880, 23275880, 23280451
Fax : 91-11-23285873
web : www.atlanticbooks.com
e-mail : info@atlanticbooks.com

ISBN 81-269-0472-0

Printed in India
at Nice Printing Press, Delhi

GENERAL PREFACE

The Atlantic Critical Studies, modelled on the study-aids available in England and America, among other places, are primarily meant for the students of English Literature of Indian universities.

However, in consideration of the local conditions and the various constraints under which our students have to study—non-availability of relevant critical books, dearth of foreign and Indian journals, inaccessibility to good, well-equipped libraries, just to mention a few of them—the models have been considerably improved upon, both qualitatively and quantitatively.

Thus, while these Studies are meant to be comprehensive and self-sufficient, the distinguished scholars who have prepared these study materials, have taken special care to combine lucidity and profundity in their treatment of the texts.

The Select Bibliography at the end is meant not only to acknowledge the sources used but also to help a student in the pursuit of further studies if s/he wants to.

Atlantic Publishers & Distributors believe in quality and excellence. These studies will only reconfirm it.

MOHIT K. RAY
Chief Editor (English Literature)
Atlantic Publishers & Distributors
New Delhi

CONTENTS

CONTENTS

INTRODUCTION

Shakespeare is the archetypal poet who speaks to us across the manifold barriers of language, space and time. Not much is known about him—it is difficult to construct a detailed biography out of the few facts that have come down to us. It is known that his plays were totally successful on the stage and also that he gained the love and respect of his contemporaries. This is not as common with poets as can be desired, for many poets lead an unappreciated life and gain fame only posthumously. Shakespeare was fortunate, for such a fate did not overtake him. His life was not a long one, but within that time he poured out a stream of poems, plays and sonnets that have hardly been equalled. There were many rules and conventions for him to follow—in technique as well as in the society he represents in his plays. Sometimes, as in *The Merchant of Venice* he followed the conventions of his time, and brought forth a unique product in which tradition joined hand with individual talent. Sometimes again, with sovereign contempt, he soared beyond all rules and regulations and still produced works that have stood the test of time—one of the tests posited by Aristotle. Each of his works is like a well-cut jewel and, viewed from different angles, the many facets of it—the plot, character, theme etc.—take on fire and light. *The Merchant of Venice* (which will be referred to as just *The Merchant* from now on) which is a romantic comedy, rewards repeated readings and scrutiny. This is because the Bard of Avon does not belong merely to Elizabethan England. He is a poet who belongs to the world and to whom the world belongs. Terms like "universality," "high seriousness," "sublimity," "tragic equilibrium," "esemplastic imagination" etc., describe only a fraction of his multi-faceted creativity. *The Merchant,* which belongs to his middle period, shows his genius at its maturest and most joyously creative stage. It contains not only one of his best-drawn heroines, but also the unforgettable and endlessly discussed character of Shylock. It captures the imagination of the young with the fairy-tale element inherent in it and creates, through pure verbal magic, a world of enchanted romantic love. At the same time the world of hard-headed commerce is also represented, with its precarious dependence on luck and on the whimsies of individual nature. Different aspects of the play will be taken up in the different chapters that follow, but, before studying the play it is necessary to know about the life of the author and his other works. Only then shall we be able to get a proper perspective to the play.

1

LIFE AND WORKS

(a) A Short Biography

A CHRONOLOGICAL TABLE OF THE CHIEF EVENTS OF SHAKESPEARE'S LIFE

1564 – Apr. 23, St. George's Day, supposed date of birth.
– Apr. 26, christening ceremony performed.

'71 – Shakespeare possibly enrolled in the Grammar School.

'78 – Reversal of fortune for Shakespeare's father.

'82 – Marries Anne Hathaway.

'83 – Birth of Susanna, first daughter.

'85 – The twins, Hamnet and Judith, baptised.

'86 – Shakespeare leaves Stratford-upon-Avon for London.

'93 – *Venus and Adonis* published.

'94 – *Rape of Lucrece, Titus Andronicus* pub.

'96 – Hamnet dies.

'97 – Buys New Place.

'99 – Buys shares in the Globe Theatre.

1602 – Buys 107 acres of land. Birth of first grandchild.

'04 – His company comes under Royal patronage and is named the King's Men.

'11 – Retires to Stratford.

'13 – *The Tempest* performed.

'16 – Jan. 25 – His will drawn up.
– Apr. 23 – Shakespeare dies.
– Apr. 25 – Buried in the chancel of Stratford Church.

Not much is known about Shakespeare's life, specially about his early life. Even his date of birth is not known for sure. But, in comparison with the other dramatists of his time, we know more about Shakespeare than about, for example, Ben Jonson or Webster. According to A.L. Rowse, this fact is in itself significant, because it is indicative of the social position of the Shakespeare family:

> That we know all this about Shakespeare is not without significance: it is due to the rootedness of the family in the neighbourhood of Stratford, his father's prominence in the public life of the little town and his own exceptional attachment to the place of his birth.[1]

One of the few reliable informations that has been handed down to us is the date of his christening. He was baptised in the parish church of Stratford-upon-Avon and in the Register of Baptism the event has been recorded thus:

> 1564, Apr. 26, Gulielmus Filius Johannes Shakespeare.[2]

This entry, made in Latin, means William, son of John Shakespeare. It should be noted here that the spelling of words was very fluid in Elizabethan England. The same word might be spelled in three or four different ways, sometimes in the same page.

A baby was usually baptised three days after its birth, so the twenty-third of April is commonly taken to be the date of his birth, the town being Stratford-upon-Avon, in the county of Warwickshire.

After this much of concrete information, the biographer of Shakespeare does not have much to rely on. It is mostly on conjecture that one has to base his biography, and this has been much lamented by those writers who undertook this difficult job. Different biographers, moreover, assign different dates to his enrolment at school, his leaving the school, going to London etc. These data, therefore, differ in the works of different biographers.

It has been conjectured, on the basis of legends and rumours, that young William had a happy and secure childhood in a prosperous family. He was the third child and the first son of his parents. His father, though not affluent, was a prosperous trader, dealing in gloves, corn and other things.

He eventually became the mayor of Stratford and Alderman in 1565 and could claim the status of a gentleman. His mother, Mary Arden, came from a family slightly higher in the social scale for they had landed property. It is true that she was not educated but it has to be remembered that in those days women, generally, did not receive education, definitely not the women from middle class families.

One of the few details that is known of his family life at this time is that his father, being the Justice of Peace and the High Bailiff of the town, was often involved in judicial matters. From this datum scholars have inferred that Shakespeare, being the eldest son, must have periodically accompanied his father to the law courts, thereby getting his knowledge of legal affairs. The best evidence of this is to be seen in the knowledge of legal affairs evinced in the Trial Scene of *The Merchant of Venice*, besides which, of course, there are numerous legal references in his works.

By this time Grammar Schools had become well-established in Elizabethan England and Shakespeare was duly admitted to the Grammar School of his village. It has become known, mainly through legends and tradition, that at this time he was about seven years old and was a sore trial to his teachers for he was by no means a good student. He, as often as not, played truant and was not interested in properly learning his lessons. Latin grammar and literature were the subjects taught in the school and Shakespeare acquired some knowledge here. Ben Jonson's comment on his "small Latin and less Greek" is well-known, but whatever small Latin he had was picked up during these school-going days. He studied here till he was about 14 or 16 years old.

Certain facts about the school and the curriculum he faced are known. The school had long hours, from six in the morning till five in the evening, with a total of about two and a half hours break spaced out throughout the day. The curriculum consisted of Latin and little else. It will be of interest here to have some knowledge of the books the young boy was likely to have read:

Poetry: *The Bucolica* of Mantuan
The Eclogues and the Aeneid of Virgil.
The Poems of Horace

The Metamorphoses of Ovid—the source of his numerous classical references.

Prose: Caesar, Livy, Cicero.

Drama: *Ten Tragedies* of Seneca.
The Comedies of Plautus
The Comedies of Terence.

Looking at this heavy curriculum, it is not surprising that one of his biographers should remark:

> Today all scholars are agreed that Shakespeare was a well-educated man of his times, that he certainly continued to further his education by wide reading throughout his life and that there is no display of learning in any one of his plays which could not have been acquired at the Stratford Grammar School.[3]

The whole idea of his having attended the Grammar School, however, has been challenged by John Dover Wilson. According to him Shakespeare's father, being a Catholic, would not have put him in a Grammar School. Instead he might have put his son in the service of some Catholic nobleman where he might have received his education, and some preliminary knowledge of acting and the lifestyle of the nobility.

It is not known for sure how long he studied at the school. There seem to have been some reversals in the fortunes of his father, the reasons for which are not known. It is definite however, that he was withdrawn from his school during his teens. At this time of life, every year at school is of crucial importance and it is not known at what age exactly he had to leave school. It could have been anything from thirteen to seventeen years.

Besides acquiring knowledge, these years at school were fruitful in other ways as well, for it was at this time that many travelling companies of players, patronised by the great Earls of Leicester, Warwick and Worcester visited Stratford. They enacted not only the old native English Morality plays and Interludes but also the Five-act plays written after the classical pattern.

A few years later an important event of his life took place. There was a village named Shottery a few miles from Stratford and there was a girl here, Anne Hathaway, the daughter of a prosperous farmer. She must have been a very charming girl, for there is a couplet, source unknown, handed down to us:

Anne Hathaway, she hath a way
To charm all hearts, Anne Hathaway.

Shakespeare fell in love with her. She was eight years older than him but this does not seem to have mattered, for he married her on Nov. 28, 1582. He was not even nineteen, while she was twenty-six. Nothing is known of the married life of Shakespeare except the fact that next year their first child Susanna was born. She was baptised on May 26, 1583. Nearly two years later the twins, Hamnet and Judith were born. They were baptised on Feb. 2, 1585. Hamnet died in 1596.

Thus, by the time that he was barely twenty-one, Shakespeare had a wife eight years older than himself, and three children to bring up. It can be surmised that he must have been worried about earning a living. Whether his married life was happy or not is not known.

There is a tradition saying that he was teaching in a school near Stratford. This detail has been handed down by John Aubrey, one of the first biographers in English Literature. There is also a widely known biographical detail of this time. It seems that, along with a few other young men, Shakespeare stole a deer from the preserves of Sir Thomas Lucy at Charlecote. It is thought that Sir Thomas ordered Shakespeare to be whipped and put in prison. It is also said that Shakespeare wrote a scurrilous ballad against Sir Thomas, and it is thought that it was because of these reasons that Shakespeare left Stratford in 1586. Whether this story is true or not is doubtful but it was circulated by the actor Thomas Betterton and also by a contemporary clergyman.

There is another story that affirms that Shakespeare had spent some years at this time as an actor in provincial companies. This idea is based on a certain will by a Lancashire gentleman in which the name of William Shakeshafte has been mentioned as a player in his service.

At about this time the theatrical group called The Queen's Players visited Stratford and this also is supposed to have influenced Shakespeare into leaving Stratford and seeking a career in London.

Not only the Queen's men, but other troupes also visited Stratford so that Shakespeare had become familiar with stage-performance from quite early in his life. In 1583 alone there were three well-known groups which played at Stratford. In 1587, which perhaps is the year in which he left Stratford, two famous and well-organised troupes visited the town. His biographers surmise that not only did he witness these plays very attentively, but had also acted in them. Hamlet's conversation with the players gives evidence of intensive first-hand knowledge of putting up a play. Perhaps he had been accepted as one of the actors in one of these travelling companies and come to London with them.

Not much is known about the period from 1586 to 1592. These six or seven years have been labelled as the Dark Years. There are many legends about these early years in London. It is said that he got a job as an assistant to the prompter in the theatre and it is also said that he eked out a living by holding the horses of the noblemen who visited the theatre. It is also thought that Shakespeare renewed acquaintance with Richard Field who had left Stratford some years ago and had become a well-established printer in London. This is quite likely because it was this Richard Field who brought out his *Venus and Adonis* and *The Rape of Lucrece* in 1593 and 1594 respectively.

Shakespeare's arrival at London, as has been pointed out, coincided with that of Marlowe who was born the same year as he himself. Apart from this, this decade of the eighties was a particularly exhilarating time. This was the time when Sir Francis Drake was scouring the Spanish Main. Sir Philip Sidney was writing his pioneering sonnet-sequence *Astrophel and Stella* and was perhaps also working on his monumental work *Arcadia*. Spenser was in Ireland, where he was writing *The Faerie Queene*. The University Wits, one by one, were converging towards London which was the centre of all activities. Lyly had already written his *Euphues* and had turned his attention to drama. He had already written two comedies, *Campaspe* and *Sappho and Phaon* which had been performed by the choir of the Chapel Royal before the Queen herself. This was in 1584. Peele, another of the University Wits, presented his charming play that was so like a modern musical, *The Arraignment of Paris*. Robert Greene, Thomas Nashe and Thomas Kyd had arrived at London. Marlowe's *Tamburlaine* was presented in 1587 and by that time Shakespeare was definitely in London. It was a time when English drama was in the making—a glorious time of exploration, in the geographical as well as literary sense. F.E. Halliday has highlighted this aspect:

> Shakespeare had arrived in London at the most thrilling moment in its history; thrilling, however, not only because danger, anxiety, expectation and hope were in the air, but also because the long awaited dramatic revival was imminent.[4]

Thus, perhaps acting minor parts in the theatre and watching plays being performed and learning his craft all the time, Shakespeare spent his first few years in London. The first mention of him that can be found is in a work by Greene which has since become famous. This is a pamphlet named *Greene's Groats—worth of wit bought with a Million of Repentance*. At the end of this there is a letter addressed to his friends Peele, Nashe and Marlowe. In it he warned them not to trust actors. He particularly mentioned a certain actor in an oblique manner who was definitely Shakespeare and thoroughly castigated him:

> Yes, trust them not: for there is an upstart crow, beautified with our feathers that with his Tyger's heart wrapt in a Player's hyde, supposes he is as well able to bombast out a blank verse as the best of you: and being an absolute Johannes factotum, is in his own conceit the only shake-scene in a country.[5]

The line "Tyger's heart wrapt in a player's hyde" is a distorted rendering of Shakespeare's line "O tiger's heart wrapped in a woman's hide" in *Henry VI*, Part III. This, together with "Shake-scene," makes one think that it is Shakespeare to whom Greene is referring. This, in turn, has made his biographers further suppose that Shakespeare, by this time, had become important enough to cause jealousy and misgivings in the hearts of these well-established University Wits. This, by itself, was no mean achievement for someone no better than a half-educated provincial, for this is how he must have seemed to them.

These years must have been, and have been taken by his critics to be, his years of apprenticeship, but they had been highly productive as well. It was during this time that he wrote the sonnets, *Venus and Adonis, The Rape of Lucrece, the Henry VI* trilogy, *Richard III, Titus Andronicus, Comedy of Errors, The Two Gentlemen of Verona* and *The Taming of the Shrew.* How successful his plays were on the stage becomes clear when one come to know from the title-page of *Titus Andronicus* (published in 1594), "as it was played by the Rt. Hon. the Earl of Derby, the Earl of Pembroke and the Earl of Sussex their servants."[6] This means that it was performed by these three well-known companies, one after the other. This list given above is significant from another point of view as well. It means that Shakespeare, unlike Kyd and Marlowe, who wrote only tragedies, could already at this early stage write successful histories, tragedies and comedies. These were his achievements by 1594, by which time Marlowe had already been killed. They prove, among other things, his versatility as a dramatist.

By the end of 1594 Shakespeare was already well-established in the group known as the Lord Chamberlaine's Men. His name occurs along with those of Will Kempe and Burbage, both famous actors, in a receipt of the Royal Treasury where all the three had been paid for having produced two plays at Queen Elizabeth's court. Having once joined the Lord Chamberlaine's Men, Shakespeare continued with them till the end of his career writing his plays only for this group.

It is thought that at about this time he paid a visit to his family at Stratford. It was a family in which the children, all grown up, were still living with their parents. Shakespeare's father was in his sixties. Shakespeare himself was only twenty-eight and his children were also growing. Susanna was nine, and the twins Hamnet and Judith were seven. Hamnet was old enough to go to school. Shakespeare stayed at home for four months. It was perhaps at this time he wrote *Richard III* and *Venus and Adonis.* The latter was dedicated to Henry Wriothesley, the Earl of Southampton, the "onlie begetter" of the sonnet-sequence that was shortly to follow.

It was in this young aristocrat, nearly ten years his junior, that Shakespeare found a patron. Not only was the Earl his patron, but, the sonnets dedicated to him have made the critics think that an intimate friendship had grown between him and Shakespeare. For a very long time it had been thought that the sonnets are not mere imaginative treatment of courtly love, but they present the true relationship between the two of them, with passionate love on the poet's part. How much of this is true cannot be proved. The sonnet also describe a Dark Lady who, along with the Earl, betrayed Shakespeare. It is a harrowing story that emerges from the sonnets. According to the sonnets, Shakespeare loved Mr. W.H., whom the critics have identified with the charismatic young Earl of Southampton, with a passionate love expressed in thc intensest manner of the tradition of Courtly Love. He was also attracted, in spite of himself, to the Dark Lady and introduced her to Mr. W.H. These two then started to have an amorous affair of their own and Shakespeare was left betrayed and alone. How much of this sordid story is true cannot be known for sure, but, however hypothetical the story might be, it should be mentioned in any account of his life. The fact that Shakespeare regarded the Earl with emotion bordering on adoration, however, can barely be doubted. He dedicated, not only the sonnets, but *Venus and Adonis* and *The Rape of Lucrece* to the Earl as well. The note of sincerity proclaims itself in the dedication to *The Rape*:

> The love I dedicate to your Lordship is without end [...] what I have done is yours, what I have to do is yours, being part in all I have, devoted yours.[7]

The story of Shakespeare's life after this is a story of success, worldly as well as literary. He bought a share in his own company and it is thought that it was the Earl of Southampton who supplied the means to do so. This definitely indicates a turning-point in his life—spelling security and prosperity:

> That Shakespeare already had sufficient wealth to join in this project would by itself make evident that he was a man of some prosperity.[8]

The lives of the poets at that time were insecure. Marlowe was stabbed to death in a drunken brawl, Greene died a poverty-stricken death. In comparison we have Shakespeare buying property:

> It meant all the difference between the dreadful insecurity poor Greene and others had died of, and having firm ground under his feet.[9]

His company, the Lord Chamberlain's Men, became the leading theatrical company and later became known as the King's Men. How successful it was can be surmised when it is known that before the end of the reign of the Queen it gave thirty-two performances at the court alone, apart from public performances. The measure of his success can be put against the proper literary perspective when it is known that he was the only dramatist to survive the terrible years of the Plague. Kyd was dead at thirty-five years of age. Marlowe, who could have been his greatest rival, was dead at twenty-nine. Greene was dead at thirty-four, Peele would die in a few years, Lyly had virtually stopped writing and so had Lodge. Nashe had become interested in pamphlet-writing. Shakespeare hardly had any serious rivals at this time. The only writer with a genius like his own, Ben Jonson, would appear a few years later. Shakespeare's star was shining the brightest.

Now, one by one, he produced the early light-hearted comedies: *A Midsummer Night's Dream, Love's Labour's Lost, Romeo and Juliet* and *The Merchant of Venice.* Shakespeare was enjoying life and literature and it is thought by many biographers that in Lord Berowne of *Love's Labour's Lost*, he has produced, as Halliday says, "a half-mocking and unconscious projection of himself." He was now, in 1595, thirty years old, fully established in a robust, joyful, creative career. It is significant that the first literary mention of his name occurs in a poem written at this time by Henry Willoughby, an Oxford undergraduate. Not only is Shakespeare, under the initials W.S., mentioned as a mentor who gives the poet good worldly advice in the matters of the heart, the writer mentions him by name as a poet:

> Yet Tarquin plucked his glistering grape
> And Shakespeare paints poor Lucrece's rape.[10]

About *A Midsummer Night's Dream* it is thought that it was produced to celebrate the marriage of the countess of Southampton, i.e. the mother of Shakespeare's patron. Queen Elizabeth was also present at the performance, which took place on the night before the wedding.

It was in 1597 that his only son Hamnet, then eleven years old, died, and no one was left to carry on the line. At this time Shakespeare was in Stratford and engaged in writing *King John*. He had, at the promptings of his father, renewed the application at the Heralds' College for the granting of a coat-of-arms. This would give the family the status of a gentleman, which, in the feudal and hierarchical society of the time, mattered a lot. This was granted and when Shakespeare came back to London, it was as a gentleman. It was at this time that he bought New Place, a fine house, the second best house in the town.

By 1598 he was so well-established that Francis Meres, in his *Palladis Tamia*, referred to him with ecstatic eloquence, comparing him with the classical poets:

> [...] the sweet wittie soule of Ovid lives in
> mellifluous and hony-tongued Shakespeare,
> witness his Venus and Adonis, his Lucrece,
> his sugred sonnets among his friends.[11]

Meres goes on to list his plays and affirms that Shakespeare is the English Plautus and Seneca in comedy and tragedy.

Not only was Shakespeare acknowledged as the best playwright of the time, his company also got a like recognition, when, in 1603 King James VI of Scotland came to succeed Queen Elizabeth as King James I of England. The Lord Chamberlaine's Men were brought under royal patronage, and became known as the King's Men. This was a significant elevation in status, for, being now the recognized servants of the King, the men of the company would wear royal livery, appear frequently at court and take part in royal pageants and processions. From now on there are many records of Shakespeare's doings. A significant information is how, in 1602, Shakespeare bought one hundred and seven acres of land for farming and again a cottage and a quarter acre of land the same year. He had continued acting in the plays staged by his company and there is a record of how he acted in Ben Jonson's play *Sejanus,* performed by the King's Men in 1603.

It is also about this time that the Mermaid Tavern became the regular haunt of the poets and the Mermaid Club was formed. One of the frequent visitors, Thomas Coryat, mentions "the worshipful fraternity of sirenaical gentlemen that meet the first Friday of every month at the sign of the Mermaid."[12] There is no record of Shakespeare being a member of the club, but he lived at lodgings only five minutes' walk from the Mermaid and must have visited it quite regularly. The poets' gatherings there have become legends.

In 1603 there was another epidemic of plague in London and Shakespeare returned to Stratford. This is the time when his great tragedies were written. *Hamlet* was performed in 1602, *Othello* was performed at court in 1604 and *King Lear* and *Macbeth* in 1606. The Problem Plays and the chronicles were also being written at this time. Keeping these plays in mind, F.E. Halliday has pointed out that the accession of King James to the throne of England was also the time for a noticeable change in Shakespeare's writings:

> [...] a change not only of matter, but of manner as well, of the dramatic medium and vehicle of his theme, for the one demanded, necessitated the other, and it is possible to make a broad distinction between his Elizabethan and his Jacobean poetry.[13]

It is quite possible that Shakespeare was writing *Measure for Measure* in the plague year of 1603. At the end of the year not only this play but also *As You Like It* was performed before the King at Wilton. This was the place where Sir Philip Sidney's sister the Countess of Pembroke lived and where Sidney had written his *Arcadia* to amuse her.

Shakespeare, by now, was dividing his time between London and Stratford, spending his summers at home. In 1608 his first grandchild was born and in the same year, towards the end, his mother passed away. Shakespeare's time in London, too, was drawing to a close, for he was to remain there for about three more years only. He now started writing the last romances. The darkness of the problem comedies and the tragedies lay in the past, the pageantry of the history plays was left behind and a serene pastoral world was being created. In 1609 the sonnets were published and in 1611 (according to Irving Ribner) he retired to Stratford. *The Winter's Tale* was performed this year.

Retirement, however, did not mean pure leisure, for he continued coming to London and getting involved in her affairs till the very end of his life. For example, he bought the Blackfriar Gate House in 1613. His name occurs in various documents every year. It is thought that *The Tempest* was performed on the occasion of a royal betrothal towards the end of 1612 and that Shakespeare himself acted in the role of Prospero. This, however, is just conjecture. In 1616 his will was drawn up and is still preserved in Somerset House. He passed away on April 23, a bare two months after he had made and revised his will.

An elaborate tomb was constructed over his grave. It has a bust of the poet writing with a quill. On the sides there are corinthian columns supporting a cornice. Over the cornice there are two allegorical figures symbolising Rest and Labour. Between these two figures there are Shakespeare's coat-of-arms and the entire thing is surmounted by a skull. There is a tablet under the bust with a Latin couplet and a sextet in English inscribed on it. Over the grave itself there is a quatrain which, it is thought, was written by the poet himself:

> Good friend, for Jesus sake forbeare
> To dig the dust enclosed here!
> Blest be the man yt spares these stones,
> And curst be he yt moves my bones.[14]

(b) Shakespeare's Works

A CHRONOLOGICAL TABLE OF SHAKESPEARE WORKS

This Table has been drawn up by Shakespeare's biographers on the basis of the entries made in the Stationer's Register, Henslowe's Diary which recorded the dates of the performances of some of the plays and certain other such sources.

Modern critics are more or less agreed on the chart that follows:

I.	1591	–	*The Comedy of Errors.*
	'92	–	*The Two Gentlemen of Verona, Henry VI, Parts I, II, III.*
	'93	–	*King Richard III, Romeo and Juliet, Venus and Adonis.*
II.	'94	–	*The Rape of Lucrece, The Sonnets, Titus Andronicus, King Richard II, A Midsummer Night's Dream, Love's Labour's Lost, King John, The Taming of the Shrew.*
	'95	–	*The Merchant of Venice.*
	'97	–	*Henry IV Part I.*
	'98	–	*Henry IV, Part II, The Merry Wives of Windsor.*
	'99	–	*King Henry V, Much Ado About Nothing, Julius Caesar.*
	1600	–	*As You Like It, Twelfth Night.*
III.	'02	–	*Hamlet, Troilus and Cressida, All's Well That Ends Well.*
	'04	–	*Measure for Measure, Othello.*
	'05	–	*King Lear.*
	'06	–	*Macbeth.*
	'07	–	*Antony and Cleopatra.*
	'08	–	*Coriolanus, Timon of Athens, Pericles.*
IV.	'10	–	*Cymbeline, The Winter's Tale, The Tempest*
	'11	–	*Henry VIII.*

Shakespeare's career has been divided into different phases by different critics. The phases are not, by any means, hermetically sealed divisions. They often overlap, so that the divisions also become blurred and indistinct. Roughly, however, as indicated in the Chronological Table given above, his career can be divided into four phases. The first phase, that of Experiment, lasts from the beginning, perhaps 1591, to 1594 or 1595. At this time he was learning his craft and mostly revising plays which were already in existence. As far as versification goes, he, during this early period, made occasional use of rhyming and end-stopped lines. There is much exuberant playing with words. The art of character delineation has not yet become remarkable in any way.

The second period, that of Development, stretches from 1594-'95 to 1601. The Chronicle Plays and the Golden Comedies belong to this period. He has attained mastery over dramatic blank verse and as far as characterisation goes, he is giving proof of insight into the psychological complexities of human beings. The plots are managed far more skillfully than in the early plays.

The third period ended in 1608. All the plays of this time show a remarkable change of mood and atmosphere. The exuberance and lightness of heart has gone, to be replaced by sombreness and a keen awareness of the existence of evil. The Great Tragedies and the Problem Plays (also known as the Dark Comedies) belong to this phase of his career.

The last period, known as his Romance period, lasted till 1612 and the four Romances were written at this time. They show a calm and serene Shakespeare, for whom evil is as much of a reality as the continuity of life is. Peace and love reach to a climax and become part of truth in these.

(c) Notes on Individual Works

THE COMEDY OF ERRORS

This is the shortest of Shakespeare's plays, and taken to be his first by many critics. It was performed at court in 1594 but whether this is the first performance is not known. The plot is taken from a play by Plautus, the *Menaechmi.* Plautus has one pair of twins but Shakespeare has two, so the cases of mistaken identities are doubled, producing hilarious laughter. Apart from the situation produced by the two pairs of twins, there is one theme that gains prominence: the relationship between husband and wife which Shakespeare was to take up again in *The Taming of the Shrew*. What is remarkable here is that the dramatist presents both the sides—that of the husband as well as of the wife, with equal sympathy.

THE TWO GENTLEMEN OF VERONA

This play is often regarded as the first of his romantic comedies. There are two pairs of lovers, two servants and two fathers. The structure is thus very symmetrical. The theme is of friendship and love in conflict with each other, with the emphasis falling on friendship. Along with this there is the theme of forgiveness and reconciliation which appears here for the first time and will go on appearing till the very end. We also have many of the features present in his mature comedies, like crossed love, disguised heroines, exile and flight. Julia is a precursor of Rosalind and Portia, just as Silvia foreshadows Juliet Lance the clown is one of those clowns who reappear again and again in Shakespeare.

HENRY VI, PARTS 1, 2 AND 3

Shakespeare's Chronicle plays are a class by themselves. No other Elizabethan dramatist wrote so many as he did. He wrote ten such plays, if *Henry VIII* is included. Not only did the pomp and pageantry of royalty captivate his imagination, but the serious issues of the duties of kings, their relationship with their subjects and their country, their human aspect—all fascinated him. Over and above everything else, it was the spirit of patriotism which inspired his creative faculty.

He based these plays on the famous *Chronicles* of Raphael Holinshed. They were performed in 1592. This trilogy was so popular that it was put on the stage three times in eight days. The trilogy presents a scene of ferocity and betrayal and ends with regicide. Greene had referred disparagingly to one of the lines in this play.

RICHARD III

This play is more of a tragedy than a history play, and the influence of Marlowe is even more marked than in the *Henry VI* trilogy. Some critics tend to group this play with the *Henry VI* plays and call the entire sequence a tetralogy. The hero, King Richard III, is a Marlovian figure, but far more complex than a typical Marlovian hero. Barring *Hamlet*, this is the longest play of Shakespeare and is extremely stage-worthy. The figure of Richard III dominates the entire play and so gives the impression of being more of a tragedy than a history play. This is the main difference between this and Henry VI.

ROMEO AND JULIET

This is centred round one of the most popular stories of the time. It is a story of family feuds and star-crossed love. As yet it is Fate, in the shape of the family feud, that controls the lives of the two lovers. The kind of tragic hero whose "character is destiny" has not yet come into being. This is because he follows the original story very closely in this play. His genius manifests itself in the speeches of great lyrical beauty and, moreover, in what was his own invention the character of Mercutio, said to be a bit autobiographical.

VENUS AND ADONIS

The story of this long narrative poem is taken from Ovid. It was such a highly successful poem that it ran through ten or eleven editions in his own lifetime. He had Marlowe's *Hero and Leander* for guidance, for narrative poetry was a new field for him. It is a highly sensuous poem and is composed in stanzas of six lines: a quatrain followed by a couplet. This is a smoothly flowing metre, highly suitable for narrative poetry and Shakespeare manages it with great artistry.

THE RAPE OF LUCRECE

This is another narrative poem based on classical myths. This poem too, like *Venus and Adonis*, was dedicated to the Earl of Southampton, professing intense love and loyalty. (*vide* Shakespeare's life *supra*). It is a sombre poem, full of the feeling of guilt. It is composed in the stanza-pattern known as rhyme royal, that is, seven iambic pentametre lines, rhyming a b ab bcc. Shakespeare manages this difficult pattern with great ease. More than the metrical achievement, it is the psychological complexities of Tarquin that raise the poem to a height far above that of a merely well-written narrative poem. Tarquin is a tragic figure.

THE SONNETS

The sonnet-sequence to Mr. W.H., named "onlie begetter," is unique. These sonnets constitute a class by themselves and are supposed to throw light on Shakespeare's relationships with his patron, who was also his friend. There are a hundred and fifty-four sonnets in the sequence, the first 126 of them addressed to Mr. W.H., who has been identified with the Earl of Southampton. The remaining twenty-eight are addressed to the Dark Lady, who has been identified with one of Queen Elizabeth's maids of honour. This in itself makes the sequence unique, for the other sonnet-sequences of the time were addressed to only one person, the poet's beloved. The sonnets throb with intense emotions like love, loyalty as well as negative ones like hatred, jealousy etc.

TITUS ANDRONICUS

This is the first of his Roman plays. It is a typical blood and thunder tragedy of the time not very appealing to modern tastes. It was a great success at the time. It follows Kyd's *The Spanish Tragedy* in structure and theme, and contains a parody of one of Kyd's most famous passages.

RICHARD II

This is the most topical of his history plays. Ireland was posing a great problem in those days and that is the theme of this play. It reflects the contemporary situation to such an extent that the Queen, after seeing it exclaimed in anger: "I am Richard II, know ye that? [...] This tragedy is played forty times in open streets and houses." The play shows the deposition of King Richard and this was such a sensitive issue that this scene had to be omitted when it was performed. The character of Richard II, which critics think is a study in weakness, is depicted with great sympathy.

A MIDSUMMER NIGHT'S DREAM

This work is definitely one of his early masterpieces. The beauty of the versification and the complexity of the plot give it a special position among Elizabethan plays. The introduction of the fairy-tale characters give it a unique significance. He is the creator of this kind of play, that is, fairy tale romance, which he will use once more in *The Tempest.* Three distinct levels have been presented here—the romantic lovers, the down-to-earth villages, and the fairies.

LOVE'S LABOUR'S LOST

This play was produced in 1594 and is remarkable for its brilliant dialogues, particularly those of Lord Berowne and Lady Rosaline. The main characters are from high aristocracy.

There are four pairs of courtly lovers and a few humble characters as well. It is in this play that the wittiest of the lords, Lord Berowne, decides to speak in simple language and denounces wit:

Taffeta phrases, silken terms precise
Three-piled hyperboles, spruce affectations
Figures pedantical: those summer flies
Have blown me full of maggot ostentation
I do forswear them.[15]

KING JOHN

This is an entirely historical play, yet, in a way, a topical play as well. It is the only play in which he has taken up the issue of religion. Just as Queen Elizabeth carried on a life-long struggle with Papacy, so did King John. Yet it is not a religious play. It is actually a patriotic play in which relations with foreign powers is the central theme.

THE TAMING OF THE SHREW

Performed in 1594, this is the first of his plays in an Italian setting. There is confidence and maturity in the delineation of Kate, the Shrew of the title, and Petruchio, the tamer. The main theme is the conflict between husband and wife as to who should gain supremacy, a very valid theme for his contemporaries. It is a rollicking and hilarious play.

HENRY IV - PARTS 1 & 2

These two parts of *Henry IV* mark the highest point reached by English historical plays. The undoubted attraction of these plays is the character of Falstaff, one of the greatest comic characters ever created. His rejection by King Henry V is one of the most moving scenes in the play. Yet the rejection is justified, for the plays are about kingship. Prince Hal could roister about with Falstaff and other cronies but when he becomes the king the burden of responsibilities fall on him and he has to close that chapter of his life. The second part thus, gains in psychological interest what it loses in comic entertainment. Falstaff, however, remains immortal. The serious issues like the duties and burdens of royalty are forgotten, and Falstaff is remembered.

THE MERRY WIVES OF WINDSOR

Queen Elizabeth was so delighted by Falstaff that she commissioned a play to be written about "the fat knight in love." This is a pure, rollicking farce and begins with Falstaff where he was left at the end of *Henry IV* Part 2. An important feature of this play is that it is thought that Shakespeare had poked fun at Ben Jonson's humour characters, particularly in the person of corporal Nym who cannot utter two sentences without using the word "humour."

KING HENRY V

This play presents Shakespeare's vision of the ideal King. Stress has been laid on the two themes of kingship and patriotism. Shakespeare, with impartial kindness, views both the sides of war—bravery, endurance and nobility on one hand, and injury, death and destruction on the other. King Henry is the ideal leader of men, inspiring his soldiers to lead them to victory. His triumph at Agincourt is well-deserved, for he pays for it, literally, with blood, sweat and tears.

MUCH ADO ABOUT NOTHING

This is one of Shakespeare's Golden comedies—a double-plotted play treating the theme of love. There is the theme of physical love which is based on external appearances, shown in the Hero-Claudio plot, and the theme of the rejection of married love, in the Benedick-Beatrice plot. The love *versus* friendship theme has been played down. His craftsmanship is also mature for, unlike as in *The Merchant of Venice*, the Benedick-Beatrice plot comes out as unquestionably more important than the tragi-comic plot of Hero-Claudio. He shows the lovers moving towards heightened self-awareness and a mature attitude towards love, as in the other romantic comedies.

JULIUS CAESAR

This is easily his most political play. It has a highly streamlined plot with very little touch of comedy. The main theme is the conflict between tyranny and liberty. Each of the characters is drawn with such care that it comes across as a living individual. It was highly successful on the stage, particularly the Forum Scene. Shakespeare had taken the story from North's translation of Plutarch's *Lives* and had adapted many of the prose passages of this book into the appropriate kind of blank verse suited to his play.

AS YOU LIKE IT

This is the happiest of his "happy" comedies, the most romantic of his romantic comedies. The main events take place in the pastoral surroundings of the forest of Arden and there are no less than four pairs of lovers, neatly married off at the end. The main theme, as in all romantic comedies, is love and it is shown here on various levels, ranging from the courtly love of Rosalind-Orlando to the more earthly love of the shepherds. Disguises provide intrigue and entertainment and in Rosalind he has given a charming heroine.

TWELFTH NIGHT

This the last of the romantic comedies. All the usual ingredients of popular plays—disguises, mistaken identities, separation and union of siblings are here, along with superb poetry and characterization. He has used a main plot with a romantic interest and a subplot with a comic one. In Sir Toby we have a later version of Falstaff and in Malvolio the puritan melancholic, already sketched in other foregoing plays, but the puritan element has been added here.

HAMLET

The first of the Great Tragedies, this is also Shakespeare's most well-known play. It is basically a revenge tragedy, but the character of Hamlet is so overpowering that this feature is often overlooked. Hamlet is not just a tragic hero whose tragic flaw is indecision, he is the typical intellectual whose appeal to modern readers is such that he has become the best known among all the tragic heroes. In this play Shakespeare shows how the blood and thunder tragedy of Kyd can become sublimated to such an extent as to leave the limitations of revenge tragedy far below and soar to inspired and universal heights.

TROILUS AND CRESSIDA

This is the first of the problem plays which are all characterized by a highly serious presentation of the less attractive traits of life and human nature, and tremble on the verge of tragedy. It is as close to a satire as Shakespeare ever came, and can be taken as a satirical treatment of the themes of war and love. Its appeal is to the intellect and Ulysses is the one character who seems to come nearest to the poet.

ALL'S WELL THAT ENDS WELL

This is another of the problem plays. It, too, has the satirical element in it but not to the extent that *Troilus* has. The basic theme is the conflict between virtue and nobility as given in the main plot of Helena and Bertram, but there are several sub-themes, like that of the conflict between old and young generations. Exposure of the braggart soldier in Parolles shows how Shakespeare has become far less tolerant of human weaknesses than he was when he created Falstaff.

MEASURE FOR MEASURE

This is the third of the problem comedies. Ironically, it is the only play besides *As You Like It* to have four marriages in it, yet the entire atmosphere is totally different from the earlier play. The motif of tricking a man into marriage is present here as in *All's Well*. The basic idea of the sovereign ruler withdrawing and disguising himself to observe the state of the country is an old theme. All the events in the play analyse the theme of justice which is one of the most prominent themes in these later plays.

OTHELLO

The second of the great tragedies, *Othello* is the first Shakespearean work of the Jacobean era. This has been called the *Romeo and Juliet* of the later Shakespeare and has also been regarded as a study in jealousy. Pathos reigns supreme, for an innocent, young and loving wife is murdered by the husband out of sheer misapprehension. The character of Iago with his "motiveless malignity" is a unique creation.

KING LEAR

This is taken to be his greatest play and has been called a Cosmic Drama, showing man's place in the universe. The story is taken from several old sources, like the old play of *King Lear, The Mirror for Magistrates* and *Arcadia*. Shakespeare wove all these diverse elements together to produce this unique play. A primitive legend is transmuted into a universal tragedy. The word used most often to describe it is "sublime". The character of the Fool in it has no parallel in other plays, for he is not only the wisest Fool, but serves many other complex purposes as well.

MACBETH

The fourth of the four great tragedies, *Macbeth* is taken to be his darkest play—a play of gloom and of horror. It is thought that, by choosing a story from the history of Scotland, Shakespeare was paying a tribute to the Scottish King James. Like *King Lear*, this, too, goes back to the legendary past and is dominated by evil. More important than anything else, Shakespeare has created a unique character, that of Lady Macbeth. The Weird sisters, the phenomenon of sleep-walking—all contribute to making the play a singularly effective one.

ANTONY AND CLEOPATRA

In this Roman tragedy Shakespeare once more turns to North's translation of Plutarch and the play is a continuation of *Julius Caesar*. The two are, however, widely different for in *Antony and Cleopatra* the theme of love predominates. It has been composed with such complexity that critics cannot agree about the genre—whether to call it a history play, a symphony, a political play, or a tragedy.

CORIOLANUS

The last of his tragedies, it has been called a political tragedy as well as a Roman tragedy. The hero is a born warrior and a patriot, but his noble nature is in conflict with society—where words are more important than action. He is rejected by the mob and he joins the enemy to bring ruin upon his country and himself. He has an uncompromising hatred and contempt for the populace and makes no secret of the fact. Such an attitude is fatal and he suffers the consequences. This play is usually grouped with the other Roman tragedies like *Julius Caesar* and *Antony and Cleopatra.*

TIMON OF ATHENS

This is an unfinished play and was never staged. As it is not a finished product, it offers interesting insights into the poet's creative processes. The play ends with the hero's withdrawal from society yet the impression that it is unfinished cannot be doubted.

PERICLES, THE PRINCE OF TYRE

Shakespeare's last period, that of the Romances, begins with this play. In these plays he is concerned with the theme of sin and repentance, followed by regeneration. These are complex themes, religious in their implications and if Shakespeare chose a story that has fairy-tale elements in it, that does not invalidate his vision. This was a very popular play and shows how Pericles lost his queen and daughter in a storm at sea and after long separation got both of them back. These themes of separation, resurrection and union will be repeated in all four of the Last Romances.

CYMBELINE

Here also the same themes (as in *Pericles*) are repeated. There is the king who loses his two sons and daughter and finds them back again after many years. Imogen the heroine is the last of the heroines to don a disguise.

THE WINTER'S TALE

This, besides having all the features of the Last Romances, is also a study in jealousy. It is also the play which has offended the neo-classicists the most, because in it he has most joyously violated the classical rules of the unities. It is clear that such external features have become insignificant for him, as he is more concerned with conveying his theme of purging a sin through repentance and rewarding through regeneration.

THE TEMPEST

This is the last of the Romances and in it Shakespeare has shown an unprecedented respect for the classical rules of the unities. All the three rules of the unities of action, time and place have been observed in it. It covers a wider range of characters than other play of Shakespeare for there are superhuman characters (Ariel) in it as well as sub-human (Caliban). The themes are the same as in the three preceding romances. It is also thought that Shakespeare put much of himself in Prospero and Prospero's renunciation of magic is Shakespeare's farewell to the theatre.

HENRY VIII

This is a history play with a difference. It is a serious play on the theme of patience in adversity. He had treated this theme in many other plays and here shows not only the King learning patience but the other characters as well. It ends on a hopeful note, assuring the continuity of life, much as the Romances do.

THE TWO NOBLE KINSMEN

This was written in collaboration with Fletcher and is a dramatisation of *The Knight's Tale* in Chaucer's *Canterbury Tales*. Shakespeare wrote the major parts of Act I and parts of Act III and V. Fletcher brought in a rather sordid subplot which Shakespeare did not like. He did not collaborate with Fletcher any more.

REFERENCES

1. Rowse, A.L., *William Shakespeare: A Biography.* London: Macmillan & Co. Ltd., 1963, 30.
2. Halliday, F.E., *The Life of Shakespeare.* London: Gerald Duckworth & Co. Ltd., 1961, 20.
3. Ribner, I., *William Shakespeare: Life, Times and Theatre.* New Delhi: Wiley Eastern Ltd., 1978, 38-39.
4. Halliday, F.E., *op. cit.*, 60.
5. Quoted in Ribner, I., *op. cit.*, 45.
6. Quoted in Rowse, A.L., *op. cit.*, 100.
7. Quoted in Halliday, F.E., *op. cit.*, 102-03.
8. Ribner, I., *op. cit.*, 50-51.
9. Rowse, A.L., *op. cit.*, 201.
10. Halliday, *op. cit.*, 118.
11. *Ibid.*, 138, Ribner, *op. cit.*, 52.
12. Halliday, *op. cit.*, 180.
13. *Ibid.*, 183.
14. Quoted in Ribner, *op. cit.*, 64, as well as many other works.
15. *The Illustrated Stratford Shakespeare.* London: Chancellor Press, 1982, 164. All quotations from Shakespeare will, from now on, be from this text.

2

THE STORY OUTLINE

The Merchant of Venice is classified as a romantic comedy, that is to say, it is a play whose main interest lies in love and marriage. The Venetian Merchant after whom the play is named is Antonio, a wealthy merchant who belongs to the high aristocratic society of Venice. He is melancholy and soberly grave in temperament and is also a man whose moral integrity is beyond question. He is also compassionate, for he helps out those who are on the verge of being ruined because of the prevalence of usury, i.e. lending money at a high rate of interest.

Antonio is extremely loyal in his friendship and this loyalty is soon put to the test. Antonio cannot only lay down his life for his friend, but when the time for doing it comes, actually does so. Shakespeare unfolds his story slowly and brilliantly and the key motive impelling the action of the play forward is revealed in the very first scene. Bassanio, Antonio's dearest friend, is a happy-go-lucky spendthrift. He spends far more than he can afford and has to borrow in order to cover his expenses. Naturally enough he has incurred many debts due to his careless way of life so that now he is in need of more money. The person to whom he owes the most is Antonio, and now he comes to Antonio again.

He however has formed a plan which, if successful, will pull him out of the morass he has fallen into. It will enable him not only to pay his debts but also to lead a life of ease and affluence thereafter.

He acquaints Antonio with his plan. There is a lovely heiress named Portia who lives in her seat at Belmont. His ecstatic description of her personality leaves one in no doubt that he is already deeply in love with her. It is also clear that it is not only her money that draws him to her. He has reason to suppose that the lady is not indifferent towards him and hopes that if he pays court to her he may be favourably received and perhaps win her:

And she is fair, and, fairer than that word,
Of wondrous virtues. Sometimes from her eyes
I did receive fair speechless messages.[1]

In order to win Portia, however, he will have to journey to Belmont with a retinue of servants whom he will have to feed, dress and pay. He will need quite a large amount of money and he hopes Antonio will help him.

Antonio, however, has invested all his property in merchandise and the ships are all out at sea. These ships, when they come back, will bring him wealth, but right at present he does not have enough money to lend Bassanio, however much he may want to. What he can do, however, is to borrow money from one of the moneylenders in the city, and pay him back as soon as his ships return home. He tells Bassanio to try to get money from the moneylenders against his name.

Bassanio then opens negotiations with Shylock, a rich Jew, asking him to lend three thousand ducats for three months, with Antonio standing as the guarrantor.

Bassanio, in looking for a moneylender, had not chosen wisely. Shylock was not the right person, for he bitterly hated Antonio. He, therefore, does not demur. On the contrary, he is elated that Antonio is standing as the guarrantor for there is the chance that Antonio's ships may not arrive on time and then he will be at his own mercy. In his heart of hearts he detests all Christians and particularly Antonio, because the latter lends money without charging any interest, thus jeopardising Shylock's own business. He hides his hatred and makes a curious proposal: he will lend Bassanio three thousand ducats for three months, Antonio standing guarantee. But, if Antonio fails to pay back within the stipulated three months, then Shylock will be entitled to take a pound of flesh from any part of Antonio's body he likes. Shylock makes it appear as though this proposal is made in a thoroughly sporting manner, as a joke between friends:

[...] in a merry sport
If you repay me not on such a day,
In such a place, such sum or sums as are
Expressed in the condition, let the forfeit
Be nominated for an equal pound
Of your fair flesh, to be cut off and taken
In what part of your body pleaseth me.[2]

Antonio falls into the trap. He himself is of an open, unsuspecting nature, and he cannot think that Shylock is being hypocritical. He truly believes that Shylock is extending a hand of friendship and he responds to this appeal to his good nature. Bassanio has misgivings, but Antonio overrules him. He is also sure that he will be easily able to pay Shylock and the bond is just a formality. The fatal bond is signed with all due legal formality.

Having obtained the money he needed, Bassanio goes to Belmont. His lively and witty friend Gratiano wants to accompany him and they go together. The action now shifts to Belmont. The first Act ends here. All the important characters have been introduced, and the action has begun. In classical terms, this Act was the Protasis. (For an explanation of this term, see Chapter 9 on Plot, *infra.*)

At Belmont, which is the seat the of Portia the beautiful heiress, there is a rather odd situation. It is more in the nature of a fairy-tale than realistic ordinary life. Portia's father was a very wise and loving father and he knew that she will be without a guardian after his death. She would also be a very rich girl and will, therefore, be besieged by undesirable suitors who will come to court her for her wealth. She herself was young and inexperienced, and may not be able to choose her husband wisely. He, therefore, devised a plan, with the intention of circumventing such a situation. He got three caskets prepared, each with a different metal—gold, silver and lead, one of which would contain Portia's portrait. The suitor will have to choose one of these. The one who chooses the right casket (that is, the one containing Portia's picture), will marry her, but those unlucky enough to choose the wrong ones will have to remain unmarried forever, throughout their lives. Many of her suitors turned away on being told these conditions, but two of them were ready to test their luck. The first of them was the Prince of Morocco. He chose the gold casket which contained the model of a skeleton. The second suitor was the Prince of Arragon who chose the silver casket which contained the picture of an idiot. Now the audience knows that it is the leaden casket that contains the picture of Portia. This is the situation obtaining at Belmont when Bassanio arrives there.

Meanwhile, another strand of the action develops. This is concerned with Lorenzo, a young Venetian, and Jessica, the daughter of Shylock. The two of them are in love, but the insuperable barrier of religion does not allow them to marry, for he is a Christian while she, being the daughter of Shylock, is a Jewess. They decide that Jessica will run away and embrace Christianity and then they will get married. Jessica disguises herself as a boy takes all the jewellery and ducats she can purloin, and elopes with Lorenzo on the evening when Shylock has gone to share a supper with Bassanio. The friends of Lorenzo, including Antonio, help him to attain his goal. Shylock is sent almost out of his mind when he discovers how his daughter has betrayed him. It is a double loss, for he has lost his daughter as well as a considerable part of his wealth, and it is difficult to say what angers him the most. The two mingle almost inextricably in a famous speech:

> My daughter!—O my ducats!—O my daughter!
> Fled with a Christian!—O my Christian ducats!
> Justice! the law! my ducats, and my daughter![3]

Bassanio, accompanied by his friend Gratiano, reaches Belmont. Shakespeare makes it clear that he has already won Portia's heart. She clearly says as much:

> Beshrew your eyes,
> They have o'erlooked me, and divided me.
> One half of me is yours, the other half yours,—
> Mine own, I would say: but if mine, then yours,
> And so all yours.[4]

She asks him to stay with her for a month or two since, if he makes the wrong choice, he will have to leave Belmont.

When he is told how he must choose one of the caskets in order to win Portia, he only wants to put his fortune to the test at once, for the more he puts it off, the more tension will there be. As Portia says, she could have helped him to choose the right casket but that would be betraying her father's trust in her, and she cannot be so dishonourable.

After much thought Bassanio chooses the leaden casket and this is the one which contains Portia's picture. The wishes of both of them are fulfilled. Portia, in a graceful speech, expresses her love for and submission to Bassanio and declares him the master of all her wealth.

It now transpires that Gratiano, Bassanio's friend, and Nerissa, Portia's companion, are also in love with each other, and with the successful outcome of Bassanio's adventure, they too declare their wishes to marry. Both Portia and Nerissa, as signs of their love, give their rings to Bassanio and Gratiano respectively, telling them to guard these rings very carefully as tokens of their love. As will be seen later, the seeds for what is known as the ring episode are planted here.

It becomes clear by now that there are no less than three pair of lovers involved here and consequently three weddings: Portia and Bassanio, Lorenzo and Jussica, and Gratiano and Nerissa.

Immediately after the revelations about Gratiano and Nerissa, the news comes that all of Antonio's ships have been wrecked, so now he cannot pay Shylock and redeem the bond. The stipulated time of three months having passed, Shylock is now insisting on holding seriously to the bond which he himself had earlier declared to have been a joke. He has now gone to the extent of imprisoning Antonio and the entire case is to be tried in the court of Venice. Antonio, certain of death, has written to Bassanio, not to come and rescue him, but to come in order to see how honourably Antonio is going to pay the dues of friendship. He wants to see Bassanio before he dies. Bassanio starts for Venice without any loss of time.

Portia now shows the strength and resourcefulness inherent in her personality. She decides that she will disguise herself as a lawyer and try to save Antonio. She sends one of her men to Dr. Bellario, a learned lawyer, to get legal advice and the lawyer's dresses she and Nerissa will need. This, however, is a secret between her and Nerissa.

Lorenzo and Jessica had come to her at the end of the casket scene and sought refuge. Now, quickly seizing on this chance, she requests Lorenzo to take care of her household. She herself, she tells him, will with Nerissa, withdraw to a monastery till Bassanio and Gratiano return. Thus, with great foresight and organizing capacity, she arranges everything. Then, accompanied by Nerissa, she starts for Venice.

Then comes the famous Trial Scene, which is easily one of the two most important scenes in the play (the other being the scene in which Bassanio chooses the casket). Everyone, including the Duke, asks Shylock to have mercy on Antonio. Bassanio offers him double the amount actually borrowed. Shylock refuses this scornfully, all the time demanding that the bond be followed.

Now Portia, disguised as a lawyer, Dr. Bellario's protegee, comes to the court, together with Nerissa, dressed as her clerk. At first, in a famous speech, known as the "mercy speech", she pleads with Shylock to have mercy upon Antonio. This is not only one of the famous speeches in this play, but in the whole work of Shakespeare:

> The quality of mercy is not strain'd.
> It droppeth as the gentle rain from heaven above
> Upon the place beneath: it is twice blessed
> It blesseth him that gives and him that takes.[5]

All her eloquence fails, for Shylock is adamant. So finally Portia asks for Antonio to be prepared, and asks Shylock if he has asked for a doctor to be present to take care of Antonio after a pound of flesh has been cut away from him. Shylock once more displays his inhumanity by replying that no such thing has been put down in the bond.

Then, as, in despair, everyone prepares for Antonio's death, Portia finally appears with her plans to save his life. She argues that the bond gives Shylock just a pound of flesh, no blood. Shylock should not shed even one drop of Antonio's blood. Realising that he is defeated, Shylock now foregoes his claim and is ready to take the nine thousand ducats that

Bassanio had offered him. Portia however, is not going to let him off the hook so easily. She says that Shylock had refused in the court to take the money and he must take the pound of flesh. Not only should he not shed a drop of blood, but he must take just a pound of flesh, neither more, nor less. Now Shylock is ready to take the original amount lent (that is, three thousand ducats only). Now Portia comes up with more laws. There is a law in Venice that any alien who conspires against the life of a citizen is liable to have all his property confiscated and also to lose his life, subject to the mercy of the duke, and of Antonio.

The tables are now turned on Shylock. The duke and Antonio forgive him without his asking them. Antonio, however, pardons him on two conditions. First that half of his property should be given to Lorenzo and that Lorenzo will be made his heir. He also asks that Shylock should convert to Christianity. Shylock, naturally, cannot do anything except agree. He is totally ruined.

The happy outcome makes the grateful Antonio and Bassanio offer remuneration to Portia, who refuses everything. Then, very naughtily, she pretends to take a fancy to the ring she herself had given to Bassanio and says she would like to have that, as a souvenir. After much verbal struggle, she manages to get the ring. Nerissa also gets her ring from Gratiano, thus providing for a later entertaining scene.

The play now draws to an end and we have reached the last Act, which is known as the "denouement". This Act consists of but one very long scene. It opens with one of the most magnificent dialogues of Shakespeare, in which the beauty of nature, youthful love and jubilant humour are inextricably mingled. Lorenzo and Jessica are waiting for Portia and Bassanio to return to their home, and Shakespeare has given the two of them some of his best poetry:

Lorenzo: The moon shines bright—In such a night as this,
When the sweet wind did gently kiss the trees,
And they did make no noise, in such a night
Troilus methinks mounted the Trojan walls
And sigh'd his soul towards the Grecian tents
Where Cressid lay that night.

Jessica: In such a night
Did Thisbe fearfully o'ertrip the dew
And saw the lion's shadow ere himself
And ran dismay'd away.[6]

Portia and Nerissa come back and are welcomed by them. Before long Antonio, Bassanio, Gratiano and others enter and a joyful reunion follows. Portia and Nerissa pretend to be angry with Bassanio and Gratiano for having given away their rings and finally Portia reveals the secret: that it was she and Nerissa, dressed as a lawyer and his clerk, who really saved Antonio. The bliss of the married couple is enhanced when it is known that Antonio, after all, had not lost his ships, for Portia had received a letter intimating the safe arrival of the ships in the harbour. Thus we have happiness for all and the reader hopes that the Recording Angel will shed a tear or two for Shylock as well. It is the most fitting end for a romantic comedy with three marriages and a happy and secure future for all. The play ends with a Senecan sentence in which love and humour mingle, for the honour of delivering the last speech (which is very much in the nature of an epilogue) falls to Gratiano:

Well, while I live, I'll fear no other thing
So sore, as keeping safe Nerissa's ring.[7]

REFERENCES

1. Shakespeare, *op. cit., The Merchant of Venice,* I.i. 162-64.
2. *Ibid.*, I. iii. 144-50.
3. II. viii. 15-17.
4. III. ii. 14-18.
5. IV. i. 82-86.
6. V. i. 1-9.
7. V. i. 306-07.

3

SCENE-WISE CRITICAL ANALYSIS

Each scene in a Shakespeare play is important. He wrote so economically that not only each scene, but each part of the scene is functional. The scenes take the action forward and each is integrally connected with the whole. In addition, there come certain high spots in the play, for some scenes are more important than the others. In our play there are two such scenes: the scene in which Bassanio chooses his casket and the one in which the trial of Antonio is held. These are known, respectively, as the casket scene and the trial scene.

It should be remembered that the plays, as originally written, did not contain any Act or scene divisions, but were written in one continuous stream. The scene and Act divisions were made by the stage-manager according to the convenience of the actors and himself. These divisions were not given by the author himself. This holds true not only for Shakespeare but for the other dramatists as well. Ben Jonson is an exception, for he had, within the plays themselves, occasionally (not always) marked out the classical plot-divisions of the play.

Act I Scene i

The first scenes of plays are usually in the nature of a prologue (consult Chapter 9 for more information on this head), as very few plays have a separate prologue preceding the play. Among Shakespeare's plays only three have a prologue specifically so designed. Three others have speeches by the chorus or other preceding the play, but not named as prologues. Very often Elizabethan and Jacobean plays have their first scenes, or part of their first scenes, doing duty for prologues. The first scene of *The Merchant of Venice* (it will be referred to as *The Merchant* from now on), is more concerned with presenting Antonio as the typical Melancholy Man of the plays of this time, than with carrying out the functions of a prologue. So here we have Antonio presented as a man suffering from a melancholy the cause of which is not known even to himself (vide Chapter 7, *infra,* Antonio's character).

This scene is marked by several distinctive characteristics, one of which is the presentation of this aspect of Antonio's character. Another important feature of the scene is that the action of the play already begins with this scene. This, though not very common, is by no means a unique feature. Comparison with the other Golden Comedies shows that the first scene of *As You Like It* also begins the action, as well as that of *Much Ado About Nothing.* In *Twelfth Night* it is only the love-lorn state of the hero which is displayed in the first scene. In our play, however, we see Shakespeare combining character-sketch along with planting the seeds of the action in the very first scene itself.

Moreover, the scene presents another aspect of Shakespeare's artistry. The melancholy man is one of the most famous and conventional figures of Jacobean plays. Shakespeare, when he wanted, could fall in with the conventions of his time in a most effective manner. Here he has suitably adapted the figure of the melancholy man as a graceful gesture to contemporary conventions, for there is no indication of any such trait in the character of Antonio in the sources he had used. Antonio declares:

> In sooth, I know not why I am so sad
> It wearies me: you say it wearies you;
> But how I caught it, found it or came by it,
> What stuff 'tis made of, where of it is born
> I am to learn.[1]

The scene shows Antonio talking to his two friends Solanio and Salarino and Shakespeare imparts to us the following facts: (a) Antonio is melancholy for no discernible reason (b) he is a wealthy man whose merchandise, loaded in many ships, is out at sea (c) he is not in love. A subtle character indeed.

Bassanio, Gratiano and Lorenzo enter. We become aware that there is a far deeper friendship between Antonio and Bassanio than between him and the two other young men he had been talking to. This relationship is put to the proof soon enough for Bassanio apprises the reader of the fact that he is a childhood friend of Antonio and has already borrowed a lot of money from him. He also makes it clear that he is heavily in debt and needs more money to pay court to Portia. The dramatist takes care to indicate that, though Portia's wealth is a consideration, yet Bassanio is attracted to her not purely through mercenary reasons. His affections are seriously engaged and he has reasons to think that she reciprocates his feelings.

Antonio, though he does not have any money at present, is still ready to stand as the guarrantor for Bassanio to any moneylender in Venice. The foundations of the two main strands of the story—Bassanio's marriage and Antonio's predicament, (to be referred to as the Casket plot and the Bond plot), are neatly laid. This is the stage which, in Indian dramaturgy, is referred to as Bindu (for more information see Chapter 13, *infra*).

This scene is entirely in blank verse, which was the staple medium of these plays. There is one feature which occurs at the end of almost every scene as it does here. The last two lines form a couplet. Usually they express an important idea, a moral message, or sum up the situation, as here. This device is borrowed from Seneca and such couplets, designated as Senecan "sententiae" usually conclude a scene or an Act (vide Chapter 11—Style, *infra*):

Where money is, and I no question make
To have it of my trust, or for my sake.[2]

Act I, Scene ii

The scene has shifted to Belmont now. In this context it is necessary to remember that one of the supposed classical requirements for plays is the unity of Place. Shakespeare's genius was not subject to any hard and fast rules and in many of his plays he flouted the classical rules. The unity of place demands that the setting of a play should be confined to one place only. Not only Shakespeare, but other dramatists also have violated these classical rules. Dr. Johnson had energetically defended Shakespeare.

It is true that drama has moved very much away from its classical progenitors in the last century or so and classical rules have become outmoded. Whereas this is perfectly true of modern plays, it should be borne in mind that the classical rules were very relevant to the Elizabethans, in fact they were the only rules the dramatist had to follow. The very fact that a defence of Shakespeare is seen to be necessary in the eighteenth century points to their relevance and their enduring quality. Such rules therefore become relevant in the context of Shakespeare's plays—far more relevant, indeed, than other modern methods such as the Marxist or other such methods which are all later products. Keeping these factors in mind, therefore, notice should be taken of the fact that the unity of place has been violated, though this should not interfere with our appreciation of the play.

The scene opens with Portia and Nerissa's conversation. The provisions and conditions of Portia's father's will are told to us. The will renders her unable either to choose her husband herself or even to refuse the man who does choose the right casket should she dislike him. Portia, a spirited girl, chafes against these restriction yet she accepts them for there is little else she can do:

> But this reasoning is not in the fashion to choose me a husband—O me! the word choose! I may neither choose whom I would, nor refuse whom I dislike, so is the will of a living daughter curbed by the will of a dead father.[3]

Nerissa names six suitors one after the other and Portia expresses her dislike for them. They, however, having come to know the conditions of the will (details given in Chapter 3, *supra*), including the proviso that they must remain unmarried if they choose the wrong casket, have decided to leave without putting their fortunes to the test. Portia is only too happy to know of this. Bassanio's name is mentioned by Nerissa and Portia reacts favourably to it: "I remember him well and I remember him worthy of thy praise."

The scene, thus summed up, is, like the former one, mainly expository in nature. All dramatists face the problem of how to impart those informations to the reader or the audience, which are important in view of the action, yet which pertain to events that have taken place before the action started or off the stage. Different plays have different methods and here the method is that of this light-hearted and witty conversation between the two girls. It may seem rather clumsy and artificial that Portia and Nerissa should talk about something they already know, however ignorant the reader may be. Here, again, the question of stage-conventions arises and the process is accepted as an usual one.

This scene is entirely in prose, in contrast to the preceding one, which is entirely in blank verse. The use of verse and prose followed different conventions which were usually accepted by the dramatists for the sake of convenience. Noble characters usually spoke in poetry and the lesser in prose, yet there were many exceptions. Such an exception has occurred here, since Portia belongs to the aristocracy and yet converses in prose. Many different explanations have been offered for this, one of which is that the prevailing tone of the scene is light-hearted and not serious. This scene, though in prose, yet has a couplet at the end, as the former one had. This Senecan sentence does not impart any moral message, but, with a humorous tolerance, sums up the situation:

Come, Nerissa—Sirrah, go before,—
Whiles we shut the gate upon one wooer, another
knocks at the door.[4]

Spoken by Portia, the sentence also serves to indicate that it has come to an end.

Act I, Scene iii

The location once more shifts to Venice. Shylock, a unique character, opens the scene by mentioning the sum Bassanio wants. He agrees to lend this amount for three months, with Antonio as the guarrantor, and as yet there is no mention of the bond. This part of the scene is in prose.

Verse is introduced with Antonio's entrance. Shylock, in a long aside, reveals his hatred for him:

I hate him for he is a Christian:
But more, for that in low simplicity
He lends out money gratis, and brings down
The rate of usance here with us in Venice.[5]

Later, as the conversation proceeds he also tells the friends how Antonio has repeatedly insulted him in public. Antonio's response to this is by no means a graceful one, for he says that he will do so again. It is now that the proposal about the pound of flesh comes up. Shylock very cunningly puts the proposal forward as if it is a friendly joke. Declaring that he would be friends with Antonio he says:

I would be friends with you, and have your love
Forget the shames that you have stain'd me with
Supply your present wants and take no do it
Of usance for my moneys.[6]

Antonio, unsuspectingly, not only accepts the offer but is convinced that "there is much kindness in the Jew." Bassanio would like to draw back, but Antonio concludes the scene with a senecan sentence, assuring Bassanio that his ships will come in a month before the term of the bond expires.

This scene is a mixture of prose and verse and it has to be noted that Antonio's entrance is accentuated by verse. There is definitely a heightening of tone at this point, as is natural with the shift from prose to verse. The couplet concluding the scene, as is natural, brings a tone of optimism. This, however, is a false and misleading optimism, for events will turn out very differently from what Antonio hopefully thinks:

Come on: in this there can be no dismay;
My ships come home a month before the day.[7]

Shylock's character, with its hatred, hypocrisy and vindictiveness, is graphically presented, as also is Antonio's frank and open nature. Antonio is incapable of hypocrisy and cannot see it in Shylock. His character is being slowly rounded out, for in the first scene the melancholy aspect and friendliness of his personality had been emphasized. Here other traits emerge. Bassanio is shown as being slightly more worldly-wise than Antonio in that he has misgivings about the bond.

Act I ends with this scene. We find that the main characters have been introduced and the action has started. The sub-plot has not yet been introduced, though a hint has been given earlier when Lorenzo, in the first scene, speaks of a meeting arranged for that evening. Of the three scenes in this Act, two are located in Venice and one in Belmont.

Portia is presented as a witty and good-humoured young girl, pliable to her dead father's wishes, however unreasonable she may think them to be. This, at present, points to one quality in her personality—her reasonableness and ability to adapt herself to circumstances. These qualities will be developed later on. In the Casket scene, for example, we shall see a display of both of these, for she will most reasonably urge Bassanio to go to Antonio's rescue as soon as possible, and adapt herself to the change.

Act II, Scene i

This scene, a very brief one (it is only forty-six lines long), only serves to introduce the Prince of Morocco who has come to try his luck with Portia. He speaks in a pompous manner, trying to excuse his complexion and create a favourable impression:

> By this scimitar
> That slew the Sophy and a Persian prince
> That won three fields of Sultan Solyman,—
> I would outstare the sternest eyes that look
> Outbrave the heart most daring on the earth
> Pluck the young suckling cubs from the she-bear,
> Yea, mock the lion when he roars for prey
> To win thee, lady.[8]

Portia, in a dignified speech, soothes his self-respect by saying that his complexion does not weigh with her. This scene does not take the action very much forward, but serves as an introduction to the Act and is a fore-runner of the Casket scene.

Act II, Scene ii

This is the first comic scene of the play. Two events happen in this scene. Launcelot Gobbo, who has been a servant of Shylock, leaves his service and joins the retinue of Bassanio, as his servant. Secondly, Gratiano obtains the permission of Bassanio to accompany him to Belmont. His motives for doing so are not explained at this stage.

This scene has two interesting features. First of all, it is a mixture of prose and verse. Launcelot and his father, as is to be expected, speak in prose. Later, when Bassanio comes in, verse is introduced, for Bassanio and Gratiano speak in poetry, for however short a time.

Secondly, it is the first comic scene of the play. In a comedy there can be serious scenes in the sense that they may not be laughter-provoking ones. In this play, for that matter, we have not had clowning scenes so far. The other scenes were not laughter-provoking ones, as the first part of this scene is. This is a feature to be kept in mind, that there are gradations among comic scenes, for there can be serious as well as clownage scenes in comedy. Comedy is meant for entertainment, not for purgation of pity and terror like tragedy. So there should be clowning or such scenes as provoke laughter. This scene is important from that point of view.

Act II, Scene iii

This is one of the shortest scenes in the play, comprising only twenty-one lines. It shows Launcelot parting from Jessica. This is Jessica's first appearance in the play. She regrets the fact that Launcelot is leaving them, but does not resent it.

The subplot starts to take shape in this scene in that Jessica sends a letter to Lorenzo through Launcelot and reveals to the audience that she is preparing to elope with him, forsake her religion and marry him. This is given in a soliloquy after the servant has departed, in a Senecan couplet:

> If thou keep promise, I shall end this strife,
> Become a Christian and thy loving wife.[9]

It is made clear now that the play has a subplot, the theme of which, as is fitting in romantic comedy, is love. As such, it parallels the main romantic plot of Bassanio and Jessica, but it does so in a minor key. It also serves to make Shylock's situation more pathetic towards the end of the play.

Act II, Scene iv

Here the carefree and gilded youth of Venice, Gratiano, Lorenzo, Solanio and Salarino, plan a masquerade in which they discuss the lack of a torch-bearer. While this discussion is going on, Launcelot brings Jessica's letter. It is promptly decided that Jessica will escape from her father's, disguised as a torch-bearer.

The scene thus takes the action of the subplot a step forward and also, incidentally, provides opportunity for one of the three disguises in the play, of which Jessica's is the first. Anticipating later events, it may be noted at present that all the three female characters of the play will be, at one time or another, donning the disguise of a male: Portia as the lawyer, Nerissa as her clerk, and Jessica as Lorenzo's torch-bearer. It has to be remembered that it was one of the common practices in these plays for the female characters to be so disguised, rendered practicable by the fact that the female roles were enacted by young boys. Not only did these disguises provide additional entertainment and add piquancy to the character, they also provided opportunities for dramatic irony and intrigue, thus enhancing the play's stage-worthiness.

Act II, Scene v

Shylock is now going for supper with Bassanio, leaving Jessica alone in the house. Jessica's concluding couplet makes it clear that she is going to take advantage of this opportunity to escape from the house. The action, thus, goes a step forward. Shylock's character reveals itself as being intolerant of youthful follies. He is alarmed at the information of the masque being organized by the young men and tells Jessica to close the windows.

Act II, Scene vi

This scene shows the elopement of Jessica. The masked young men are outside Shylock's house. Jessica appears at the balcony and, reassured by Lorenzo's presence, hands him the casket containing her jewellery. She shows a little bit of uncertainty at first, crying out:

> Lorenzo, certain, and my love indeed
> For who love I so much? and now who knows
> But you, Lorenzo, whether I am your?[10]

Lorenzo reassures her, and later, when she goes in (that is, out of the balcony in order to come out at the door) his description of her makes us sure of his sincerity:

Beshrew me, but I love her heartily
For she is wise, if I can judge of her
And fair she is if that mine eyes be true
And true she is, as she hath proved herself.[11]

Finally she comes down and joins him.

The Elizabethan stage had a balcony at the back and the dramatists made extensive use of this feature in their plays. The Balcony-scene in *Romeo and Juliet* is a famous example.

Act II, Scene vii

This is the scene in which the Prince of Morocco chooses his casket. Shakespeare has given more stage-time to this prince than to the one from Arragon, for the Prince of Morocco appears in two scenes whereas the Prince of Arragon comes in only one. The business of choosing starts at once as the scene opens, without any preliminaries. The Prince advances many arguments and finally chooses the golden casket, which bears the legend "who chooseth me shall get what many men desire." He thinks that everyone will desire to have Portia, and, also, gold is the only metal worthy enough to hold her portrait within itself. He opens it and finds the image of a skeleton inside, with an appropriate scroll.

It has to be borne in mind that there are three casket scenes in the play, for the three caskets and the three suitors, but it is the one in which Bassanio chooses his casket which is usually designated as the casket scene. There are certain important aspects of the scene which will be pointed out later in the analysis of the second scene of the third Act which is the one where Bassanio chooses his casket. This present scene itself provides dramatic suspense and tension, for the audience also does not know what each casket contains. The sympathy of the audience is with Bassanio, so when the golden casket reveals the skeleton we heave a sigh of relief. Not only does the scene create tension but it also resolves the tension and, moreover, acquaints the reader with the contents of the golden casket. In addition, the scene also presents the element of spectacle (opsis) which is one of the classical requirements of drama as given by Aristotle.

Act II, Scene viii

This scene is a dialogue between Solanio and Salarino. No action takes place, but the reader comes to know of three important things. First of all Bassanio has set sail for Belmont, secondly Lorenzo and Jessica have managed to escape from Venice, and thirdly Antonio's ships have foundered. Shakespeare imparts all these pieces of information in a short scene of only fifty-three lines, in a very economical manner. Yet the order in which these informations are given should be noted: first there comes the news about Bassanio and Gratiano—an information that does not evoke much emotion. The second information contains mainly the element of laughter, for Solanio describes Shylock's reaction to Jessica's flight in a highly comical manner, not with any sympathy:

I never heard a passion so confused,
So stranger, outrageous and variable
As the dog Jew did utter in the streets:
My daughter!—O my ducats!—O my daughter!
Fled with a Christian!—O my Christian ducats.[12]

The third news about Antonio's loss of his ships is a very serious piece of news, for it at once creates suspense about the bond. Shakespeare, thus, has mingled the elements of laughter and of serious tension in the same scene. These two characters, Solanio and Salarino, carry out the function of the chorus in giving us the news.

Act II, Scene ix

This is the second of the three scenes in which a suitor of Portia makes a choice between the three caskets. Here it is the Prince of Arragon who faces the challenge. Unlike the Prince of Morocco, he appears only once, in this scene. This character is usually depicted on the stage as a self-important fool and this interpretation is justified by his action. He chooses the silver casket on which is written "who chooseth me shall get as much as he deserves." The Prince is foolish enough and vain enough to think that he deserves Portia. When he opens the casket, however, all he finds is "the portrait of a blinking idiot." He shows a grain of sense when he says:

Still more fool I shall appear
By the time I linger here
With one fool's head I came to woo
But I go away with two.[13]

After his departure Portia is told of the arrival of a young Venetian Lord whom the reader, as well as Nerissa, at once take to be Bassanio. The critical observations about the scene in which the Prince of Morocco makes his choice apply to this scene also.

This scene ends the second Act, and is far longer than the first. Whereas Act I contains only three scenes, this Act has no less than nine. In fact it is the longest of the Acts and the only one to contain so many scenes. Many important events happen in it but the two most important scenes are still to take place. Shakespeare has dispensed with the less important works to be done and clears the stage for the main action. According to the classical rules of dramaturgy, this Act will form part of the Epitasis (vide Chapter 9—Plot, for more information).

Act III, Scene i

We have now travelled midway through the play. Events now come thick and fast, one upon the other. In this scene we come to know with certainty about the wreck of one of Antonio's ships from the conversation between Solanio and Salarino. Again as in former scenes, these two characters function like the chorus in that they convey important news through their dialogue.

This is the scene which contains Shylock's famous speech. He comes on the stage and accuses the two young men of having known fully well about Jessica's elopement. The two of them, far from being shamefaced about it, mock him. At this he bursts out, in fully justifiable anger and chagrin:

> Hath not a Jew eyes? Hath not a Jew hands, organs, dimensions, senses, affections, passions? Fed with the same food, hurt with the same weapon, subjected to the same diseases, healed by the same means, warmed and cooled by the same winter and summer, as a Christian is? if you prick us, do we not bleed? if you tickle us, do we not laugh? if you poison us, do we not die? and if you wrong us, shall we not revenge?[14]

We have seen him before this as a hypocritical and vindictive man in the third scene of Act I. He has been described comically as a man to whom gold is as important as his own daughter (Act II Scene viii). Now a different dimension is added to his character, for he is elevated into the representative of a persecuted race. This is particularly the reaction of modern readers, who have come to live with the memory of the aftermath of Hitlerian atrocities, though it was not so effective in Shakespeare's own times. A Jew, at that time, was looked upon as very near an ogre, so it becomes all the more awe-inspiring to think of our dramatist being able to consider him sympathetically. With him it is not the style that makes the man, but this ability to see into the inmost recesses of a man's mind and then portray it with sympathy that makes him so great.

Act III, Scene ii

This is the fateful scene in which Bassanio makes his choice among the caskets, and therefore it has come to be designated as the casket scene. It is so known despite the fact that there are two other scenes before this in which two other princes have tested their fortunes in like manner.

The scene opens with a speech by Portia in which she pleads with Bassanio to stay for a month or two with her before putting his fate and ingenuity to the test. Playfully, in a captivating manner, she as good as tells him that she loves him:

> Beshrew your eyes
> They have o'erlooked me and divided me:
> One half of me is your, the other half yours,—
> Mine own, I would say: but if mine, then yours,
> And so all your![15]

Bassanio, however, is on tenterhooks, for he does not like the torture of uncertainty. Portia can tell him which casket contains her portrait, but that will be highly dishonourable, so she can but possess her soul in patience and wait for him to make up his mind. She however, gives him a clue by having a song sung of which the first three lines rhyme with the word "lead" and at the end there is repeated reference to death and knell or the tolling of a bell. These also are associated with lead which was used to make coffins with. It is not clear whether Bassanio at all takes this hint or even listens to the song with attention. He delivers a speech in which he presents his arguments against gold and silver, and in favour of lead. Then he chooses the lead casket which, as the audience knows, contains Portia's portrait. Now Portia, in accordance with all the requirements of the social customs of maidenly modesty, declares her willing acceptance of Bassanio as her husband:

> Myself and what is mine, to you and yours
> Is now converted: but now I was the lord,
> Of this fair mansion, master of my servants
> Queen o'er myself; and even now, but now
> This house, these servants and this same myself,
> Are yours, my lord.[16]

She gives him her ring as a token, adjuring him never to part with it if he loved her.

Gratiano and Nerissa now declare that they too, love each other and want to marry. They had been waiting for the successful outcome of Bassanio's fortunes to make public their own liking for each other.

Before marriage celebrations can begin, Lorenzo, Jessica and Solanio come in. Lorenzo and Jessica have come to seek refuge till they can settle down in their own home, though this is not made clear. Far more important is the news brought by Solanio, who has brought a letter from Antonio. The letter confirms our worst fears, for it tells Bassanio that Antonio is awaiting trial. He has not been able to repay Shylock within time for each one of his ships has been wrecked. He wants Bassanio to come to Venice, not to rescue him, but to see how honourably Antonio is paying the forfeit.

Portia, to whom the situation is explained, shows her warm-hearted generosity by at once offering all her wealth freely to save Antonio:

> You shall have gold
> To pay the debt twenty times over.[17]

She urges Bassanio to start as soon as possible for Venice, after they have got married.

This scene is the second most important scene in the play. It is also the second longest scene, containing as it does three hundred and twenty-five lines as against the Trial scene's (which is the longest scene in the play) four hundred and fifty-seven lines. The Trial scene, of course, is the most important, but this is no less important, for this is the culmination of the casket plot, as the Trial scene is the culmination of the Bond plot. It creates and resolves suspense most successfully and also provides dramatic irony, for everyone except Bassanio knows what the different caskets contain. It also contains the element of spectacle (opsis), which according to Aristotle, is the sixth requirement of a play. Out of the two important plots the play deals with, the one related to the theme of love (which is the most important theme in a romantic comedy) comes to a happy resolution.

The scene, however, is much more than a merely romantic scene, for, with the coming of Antonio's letter, there comes a turn in the tide of events. Suddenly the mood becomes serious. One is transported, as it were, from the fairy-tale world of romantic love to the commercial world of usury and forfeiture. The two plots are strongly knitted together.

The casket scene has intrigued Shakespeare's critics very much and many different interpretations are to be found. It has been pointed out that the dramatist has stated here the problem of judging by appearances. This is an age-old problem which each individual must tackle for himself. Shakespeare presents the problem in a dramatized and glorified form so that it affords entertainment as well as food for thought.

The story has distinct elements of the fairy-tale in it and this has been noticed and commented upon. The story of making a choice out of three is to be found in many fairy-tales and myths. The myth of how the golden apple was accorded to Venus by Paris is one such example, for Paris had to give the apple to one out of three goddesses. Shakespeare himself will make use of this idea again in *King Lear* in which the King divides his kingdom among his three daughters. Such a matter of choice is always related to morality. For example one brother (usually the youngest) is chosen out of three by a benevolent fate and it is usually seen the selected one deserves the favour, for he is kind and generous, though he may be a fool in the eyes of the world. One of the sources of this story is the *Gesta Romanorum* (see the section on sources, Chapter 9, *infra*) where a girl has to make the same kind of choice in order to win a husband. Shakespeare has inverted the story for here it is a man who has to make the choice, and the same choice is made.

The story has, apart from these fairy-tale dimensions that give it literary depth, great possibilities on the stage. It offers the element of spectacle not once, but three times, much opportunity for good acting and also scope for good direction and stage-management. It is also to be noticed that the only song in the play occurs in this scene. In other words, this scene offers the only scope for vocal music. There is also dramatic irony in the fact that Bassanio has been able to come to Belmont with the gold which Antonio has risked his life to get for him, and yet he decries gold when he has to make his choice. There are, thus, two kinds of dramatic irony involved when he makes the choice. First is the simple one that everyone save him knows the secret of the caskets, and the second is the satirical and sombre one that, though he rejects gold, yet it is because of the gold borrowed at so much cost that he has been at all able to come and court Portia. Along with this goes the thought that Bassanio is a spendthrift, he is in great need of gold as he has debts everywhere, so it is not very natural for him to reject gold in the way he does.

Act III, Scene iii

This scene, taking place on a street in Venice, only serves to highlight Shylock's determination to have his pound of flesh. Antonio has to undergo the ignominy of being imprisoned. Once more the vengefulness of Shylock is contrasted with the generous self-sacrificing friendship of Antonio. He clearly says that he wants Bassanio to come, not to rescue him, but only to see how honourably Antonio can pay his debts:

> Pray God, Bassanio come
> To see me pay his debts, and then I care not.[18]

Act III, Scene iv

This is the scene in which we see Portia making provisions for guarding her household while she goes to Venice in order to rescue Antonio. She hands over the management of her house to Lorenzo and then she reveals her plans to Nerissa and also to the audience. She sends an efficient and trusted servant to her cousin, the learned Dr. Bellario at Padua from whom she hopes to get legal advice as well as the clothes she needs in order to execute her plan.

The scene unfolds the character of Portia in many ways. She makes the plans to go to Venice single-handed, for she does not consult Nerissa but informs her of her own decisions after having made all the necessary arrangements. Lorenzo has come to her place purely by chance, and she is quick to use this coincidence to make him look after her household. As we see, forethought, the ability to take quick decisions, the shrewdness to implement that decision—all these qualities have been bestowed on her by the dramatist. Yet the decision does not weigh heavy on her, nor is she worried, for everything is done in a light-hearted, sportive spirit. She jokes with Nerissa:

> I'll hold thee any wager
> When we are both accoutred like young men
> I'll prove the prettier fellow of the two;
> And wear my dagger with the braver grace.[19]

Act III, Scene v

This is a light-hearted scene between Jessica, Launcelot and Lorenzo. It serves to bring the Act to a close, highlights the married bliss of Lorenzo and Jessica and also acquaints the reader with Jessica's opinion of Portia. Shakespeare's heroine has such an endearing charm that not only men, but women also appreciate her. Jessica's admiration for Portia is entirely ungrudging, generous and free from jealousy. This affords us an insight into Jessica's own nature, which is thus seen to be generous and free from meanness.

Act IV, Scene i

This is easily the most important scene of the play, known as the Trial scene. Antonio is brought for his trial at the Venetian court. The Duke himself requests Shylock to have mercy on Antonio, and Bassanio is ready to pay double the amount actually borrowed. Shylock turns a deaf ear to all pleas and refuses the amount offered. It seems as though there is nothing to be done when Nerissa, dressed as a lawyer's clerk brings a letter of recommendation from the learned Bellario, introducing his young protégé, who is none other than Portia in disguise. Portia, disguised as a lawyer, comes in. She pleads with Shylock to have mercy. This is one of the most famous passages of the play:

The quality of mercy is not strain'd
It droppeth as the gentle rain from heaven
Upon the place beneath; it is twice blessed:
It blesses him that gives and him that takes.[20]

The speech, known as the "mercy speech," goes on to equate the merciful man with God himself. She gives Shylock every opportunity to relent gracefully and offers him three times the sum owing to him. All this to no avail. Tension mounts as she tells Antonio to prepare himself. Shylock is shown as quite inhuman in his vengefulness when he refuses to provide for a doctor to minister to Antonio.

Finally the turning-point comes with Portia declaring that Shylock must take his pound of flesh without shedding any blood. She further adds that he must take just a pound of flesh, neither more, nor less.

There is jubilation in the court. Things take a turn for the worse for Shylock and he first becomes ready to take three times the amount as had been already offered by Bassanio, and then to take just the original amount and give up the case. But he had been clamouring for justice up till now and Portia says he must have justice and take only his pound of flesh. A defeated Shylock is now glad enough to give up all his claims, but this is only the beginning of his misfortunes. Portia now reveals how according to another law if any alien tries even indirectly to take the life of a Venetian, half of his wealth goes to the intended victim and half to the state, and his life lies in the hands of the duke.

The duke grants him pardon without being asked and Antonio gives up his share of Shylock's wealth on condition that it will go to Lorenzo and that Shylock be converted to Christianity.

The serious business of the scene being over, Shakespeare now turns to lighter matters. Portia refuses the gift of three thousand ducats and wants the ring she had given to Bassanio in the Casket scene. Bassanio does his best to fob her off and finally tells the truth:

> Good sir, this ring was given me by my wife,
> And when she put it on she made me vow
> That I should neither sell nor give nor lose't.[21]

She pretends to be angry at Bassanio's refusal and leaves the court, at which Bassanio sends Gratiano with the ring.

This Trial scene, like the Casket scene, has been analysed and interpreted in many different ways by literary critics. From the point of view of plot-construction, it can be asserted that this is the climax or the *summa epitasis* of the plot. (For clarification see Chapter 9, *infra*). The two stories, also, that of Bassanio and of Antonio, both come together in this scene. Suspense and dramatic irony is created with great skill. Suspense is there in the circumstances of the trial itself, till Portia turns the tables, and dramatic irony because the audience knows the lawyer and his clerk to be Portia and Nerissa in disguise and this dramatic irony affords the maximum entertainment in the ring episode. As has often been seen before this, Shakespeare mingles the serious and the light-hearted in this scene. Before Portia's introduction of the legal quibble, the scene, indeed the entire play, trembles on the verge of tragedy, then, after the "volte" or the turning-point, there is the light-hearted comedy of the ring.

It should also be noted that in this scene Portia acts as the *deus ex machina*, resolving all problems and giving a happy ending to the play (for explanation of this term see Chapter 9, *infra*).

Her disguise and that of Nerissa, it should be remembered, provide another instance of how Shakespeare makes use of popular conventions and devices to provide entertainment and dramatic irony. As young boys used to play female roles at that time, such disguises were very popular. Many of Shakespeare's heroines make use of disguises for various reasons. Viola, Portia, Rosalind and Imogen are the most important of them. In each case, circumstances fall out in such a manner that the heroine has to don a disguise. The difference in this case is that whereas the other heroines take to disguising themselves in order to procure safety for themselves, no such selfish motive impels Portia. She dons the disguise in order to save Antonio. From this point of view she is unique.

No less than three such disguises occur in this play. Jessica disguises herself as a young boy in order to be united with her lover. Portia disguises herself as a lawyer out of pure humanitarian motives of saving Antonio and Nerissa dons the disguise of her clerk in order to accompany and support Portia. Shakespeare has used the same device in three different ways to serve three different purposes. This features, alone, shows how far Shakespeare had progressed in his art by the time he came to write these comedies.

Act IV, Scene ii

This is the shortest scene in the play, containing only nineteen lines. In it Gratiano comes and gives Bassanio's ring to Portia. Nerissa goes with him to Shylock's house and resolves that she too will get her ring from him. Foundations are thus laid for the entertaining scene later. This brief scene serves to bring this Act to a neat conclusion.

This Act is itself a short one, containing only two scenes. One of them, the Trial scene, is the longest scene in the play, containing four hundred and fifty-seven lines, and the other is the shortest, having only nineteen lines. Its importance however is not diminished because of this, for not only does the Act bring the Epitasis to an end, but the Trial scene is the *summa epitasis* of the play. This is the point at which events reach such a height of complexity that tension is at its peak, and, in a comedy, a tragic outcome seems to be unavoidable. These difficulties, in the present case, are smoothed out by Portia who comes as the *deus ex machina*.

Act V, Scene i

This scene is the only scene in this Act. The very first lines of this concluding scene takes us to the world of the moonlit enchantment of romantic love, as opposed to the world of commerce and legal complexities of the preceding Act. In fact, throughout the play, there is this transition from the world of commerce to the world of romance, that is, from Venice to Belmont. Nowhere is this shift so well-marked as here. The world of commerce has been seen at its most complex and now the world of romance is seen at its most enchanting and this is the mood that closes the play.

Lorenzo and Jessica are waiting for the return of Portia and Bassanio and it is a moonlit night. The two of them talk about other moonlit nights which were highly conducive to love and romance. They outdo each other in no less than seven alternating passages. Each of these passages takes an instance from Greek mythology, mingling natural beauty with the potent magic of youthful love:

Lorenzo: The moon shines bright—In such a night as this,
When the sweet wind did gently kiss the trees,
And they did make no noise, in such a night,
Troilus, methinks, mounted the Trojan walls,
And sigh'd his soul towards the Grecian tents
Where Cressid lay that night.

Jessica: In such a night
Did Thisbe fearfully o'ertrip the dew;
And saw the lion's shadow ere himself,
And ran dismay'd away.[22]

The element of humour also comes in, particularly in the last passage spoken by Jessica:

Lorenzo: In such a night
Did pretty Jessica, like a little shrew
Slander her lover, and he forgave it her

Jessica: I would out-night you, did nobody come;
But hark, I hear the footing of a man.[23]

The news that Portia is to arrive shortly brings about a very brief break in the enchantment, but then it is reinforced by two fine speeches by Lorenzo about music. Portia's arrival, with her down-to-earth and humorous comments serve to furnish a realistic tone. Then Bassanio, Antonio and the others arrive and there is joyful reunion.

Soon enough, however, the attention of the principal characters is diverted by a quarrel between Gratiano and Nerissa about the ring. Both the husbands are berated by the wives for the two naughty girls pretend to think that their husbands had given the rings to other girls. Finally all is revealed, to the wonder and amazement of the male characters.

There are more revelations besides the secret of how Portia saved Antonio, for Portia has received the news that three of Antonio's ships have returned safely to the harbour, laden with rich merchandise, and Nerissa gives Lorenzo the deed of gift signed by Shylock. This deed of gift endows Lorenzo with Shylock's wealth. The play now ends with a senecan couplet, a humorous one in keeping with the happy ending. It occurs in a speech by Gratiano. Just as the play does not have any prologue as such, it does not have any epilogue so designated either. Instead there is a short speech, neatly concluding the play with a reference to the ring episode:

Well, while I live I'll fear no other thing
So sore, as keeping safe Nerissa's ring.[24]

This is the only scene of this Act and concludes the play in a fitting manner. In classical terminology, it is the "catastrophe" or the denouement where all the strands of the story are taken up and neatly woven together to reach the desired end of the play. In the case of romantic comedy this end is a succession of happy marriages and here we have three pairs of lovers neatly married off. Shylock is the only character not present in this scene. He belongs to the commercial world symbolised by Venice and the doors of the world of love have shut him out. Antonio is present, but he has not been paired off with any female character. This fact, again, has been highlighted by many critics and stage-directors who show him standing outside the lighted house of Portia at the end.

REFERENCES

1. *The Merchant of Venice*, Act I, sc. i, ll. 1-5.
2. Act I, sc. ii, ll. 184-85.
3. Act I, sc. ii, ll. 20-25.
4. Act II, sc. ii, ll. 131-32.
5. Act I, sc. iii, ll. 41-44.
6. Act I, sc. iii, ll. 137-40.
7. Act I, sc. iii, ll. 179-80.
8. Act II, sc. i, ll. 24-31.
9. Act II, sc. iii, ll. 20-21.
10. Act II, sc. vi, ll. 29-31.
11. Act II, sc. vi, ll. 52-55.

12. Act II, sc. viii, ll. 12-16.
13. Act II, sc. ix, ll. 70-73.
14. Act III, sc. I, ll. 57-64.
15. Act III, sc. ii, ll. 14-18.
16. Act III, sc. ii, ll. 66-71.
17. Act III, sc. ii, ll. 305-06.
18. Act III, sc. iii, ll. 35-36.
19. Act III, sc. iv, ll. 62-65.
20. Act IV, sc. i, ll. 183-86.
21. Act IV, sc. i, ll. 441-43.
22. Act V, sc. i, ll. 1-9.
23. Act V, sc. i, ll. 20-24.
24. Act V, sc. i, ll. 306-07.

4
THE MAJOR THEMES

One of the prime requirements for any play is that it should have a central theme around which the work should be constructed. Very often it is the theme that gives unity to an otherwise sprawling work. Shakespeare's works are not sprawling, but they touch so many spheres of life that often it is difficult to say for certain what the unifying theme of a play is. *The Merchant* also presents great complexity in this regard. It is classified as a romantic comedy and the main theme of such a play is love and marriage. All the romantic comedies of Shakespeare, *The Merchant, Much Ado About Nothing, As You Like It* and *Twelfth Night,* conform to this rule and end with multiple marriages. There are three marriages in our play. It would seem that love is the undisputed theme in this play. This itself has been looked at from many different angles and, in addition, many critics have thought of other themes for the play. Even these latter, however, concede that love is the main theme.

The theme of love is so very clear that it hardly needs to be clarified. All the same, in contrast with the other comedies, this theme is at times eclipsed by the story of Shylock and his pound of flesh. This is the reason why, in comparison with the other golden comedies there is more variety in critical opinions about the theme. First of all, it will be necessary to look at the theme of love itself in brief.

The Theme of Love

Analysing the special features of romantic comedies, H.B. Charlton points out that, first and foremost, it is the prevalence of love as the theme that marks out such comedies:

> Romantic comedy is pre-eminently the comedy of love. It is its specific occupation with wooing which distinguishes it most markedly from classical or Roman comedies.[1]

Love as it exists in romantic comedies has certain distinctive features. It is present in classical drama also, but in such plays love-intrigues are dealt with in a rather casual manner. In romantic comedies love is taken very seriously. A maiden has to be courted and won. Her love is to be attained with difficulty and treasured with care. Love itself has become an intense emotion, almost transforming the lover, turning him into a better and nobler person who is ready to make sacrifices for love.

This change in the attitude to love, which changed the genre of romantic comedy itself was brought about by the introduction of the idea of courtly love and chivalry:

> Dante had transmuted womankind for men. He had opened their eyes to the image of woman whose coming is as from heaven to reveal a miracle.[2]

Elizabethan romantic comedy follows this attitude to love and it is this serious intense love which is the theme of *The Merchant*. If the different stories told in the play are considered one by one it will become amply clear.

There are three pairs of lovers in the play, the most important being the pair of Portia-Bassanio. We see that Bassanio is ready to sacrifice everything for love, for he chooses the lead casket which bears the motto: "who chooseth me must give and hazard all he hath." Thus in choosing this casket he proves himself ready to give all and to risk all without any certainty of getting any return. This is the basic idea behind courtly and romantic love. Such love is selfless and all sacrificing. The lover should feel highly favoured that he is allowed to love the divine creature that his beloved is, without the hope of being loved in return. Bassanio's description of Portia makes this attitude clear:

> And she is fair, and fairer than that word,
> Of wondrous virtues [...]

[...] Nothing undervalued
To Cato's daughter, Brutus's Portia;
Nor is the wide world ignorant of her worth.[3]

Bassanio's love, however, is not hopeless love, for, as he says, he had received "fair speechless messages from her eyes," and therefore, hopefully, he goes to court her and is successful in winning her.

As far as Portia herself is concerned, she too is deeply in love with Bassanio, though in maidenly modesty she cannot openly talk about the intensity of her regard. Her attitude when she is hesitating about the caskets points out the agonized state of her mind:

[...] with much, much more dismay
I view the fight than thou that mak'st the fray.[4]

She is on tenterhooks. Then when he makes his choice she exclaims:

O love! be moderate, allay thy ecstasies
In measure rain thy joy, scant this excess
I feel too much thy blessings; make it less
For fear I surfeit.[5]

Thus we see that romantic love has spread its enchantment over her too and she is as intensely in love as her suitor is.

The second pair of lovers, Lorenzo and Jessica risks all, much more so than Bassanio does. He has only to choose between the caskets and, on failing, has to remain celibate throughout his life, but Jessica has to leave the security of her father's house and the sanctity of her religion and has to face an unknown future. Lorenzo also is worthy of this intense all-sacrificing love, for he is quite aware of her worth. He exclaims, like any Petrarchan lover "Beshrew me, but I love her heartily," and goes on to extol her wisdom and virtue:

For she is wise, if I can judge of her,
And fair she is, if that mine eyes be true
And true she is, as she hath proved herself
And therefore like herself, fair, wise and true
Shall she be placed in my constant soul.[6]

Shakespeare does not give much importance to the third pair of lovers, Gratiano and Nerissa. But there is never any doubt of the depth of their love. Gratiano is a light-hearted, happy-go-lucky fellow, but he has hidden depths in his nature that Bassanio did not know of. He had waited to see how Bassanio fared, then only did he make his own affairs public:

You saw the mistress, I beheld the maid;
You lov'd, I lov'd, for intermission
No more pertains to me, my lord, than you.
... ...
I got a promise of this fair one here
To have her love, provided that your fortune
Achieved her mistress.[7]

Their love for each other has survived the test of separation for "intermission" did not matter to Gratiano, and also the obstacle of the uncertainty of Bassanio's fortunes. They had the patience and the loyalty to wail till Bassanio's and Portia's fates were settled.

It can be pointed out that we have romantic love in the play in three different ways in the three pairs of lovers. We see its most intense manifestation in Bassanio and Portia, with duty, honour, loyalty, devotion all enhancing the value of this love. There is a more light-hearted treatment in the affair between Lorenzo and Jessica. In their case love does not manifest itself in intense poetry and language, but actions speak louder than words and their elopement, involving the change of religion, is proof enough of the serious quality of their love. The most light-hearted pair is the one of Gratiano and Nerissa, but in them, also, there is depth and sincerity.

We find a different kind of love in the friendship between Antonio and Bassanio. Though not romantic love, yet it is love of a pure and selfless kind where each is ready to risk not just material property but to lay down his life for the other. Their friendship is like the classical friendship of Damon and Pythias who were each ready to forfeit their life in order to save the other. Though it is romantic love which is the main theme of romantic comedies, this love, too, should not be neglected, but considered in full seriousness.

Besides this all-important theme of love, several other themes have also been perceived by literary critics at different times. These will now be explained.

The Theme of Right and of Justice

It is thought that Shakespeare's intention in this play was to explore the themes of parental and legal rights and justice. It was the critic Hermann Ulrici who first expounded this idea:

> Human life is considered as a transaction of business, with right or justice as its foundation and centre.[8]

Looked at from this point of view, in the play Portia's father is seen to have exercised his parental rights and devised a way for limiting his daughter's rights in a drastic manner. First of all, Portia will have to marry the man who chooses the right casket, her own inclinations do not matter at all; she will have to marry him even if she dislikes him. Secondly if she happens to love the man who chooses the wrong casket, she will not be able to marry him. Thirdly, if no one is ready to try his luck or if everyone chooses the wrong casket, she will have to remain unmarried throughout her life. She mentions these drawbacks in the second scene of the first Act:

> I may neither choose whom I would; nor refuse whom I dislike; so is the will of a living daughter curbed by the will of a dead father.[9]

This point, however, is not laboured in the play, but the question arises: should the parents' right be so absolute as to curb the rights of the children? Portia is a very dutiful child and every time a suitor tries his luck she assures him that she will marry him if he chooses the right casket, but the reader knows that she does not like the Prince of Morocco or the Prince of Arragon. On the other hand, she definitely likes Bassanio. Her future, therefore, is very precariously balanced. As it is, everything falls out just right, for the play is a romantic comedy, but it could easily have been all ruined. Parental right is brought into question in the play.

The exact opposite of Portia's situation is seen in the subplot of Lorenzo and Jessica. The Jew Shylock, after all, is a far more considerate parent than the Christian father of Portia, for he does not exercise as much restraint on Jessica as the latter does. Yet Jessica is a far less obedient daughter than Portia, and elopes with Lorenzo. This is a direct flouting of parental authority, yet, in the happy world of romance the outcome is the same. Both Portia and Jessica get their heart's desire. Lorenzo and Jessica, in addition, get the wealth of their father.

The question of legal rights is again another important theme of the play. Just as the theme of parental rights is concerned with Portia, so the theme of legal rights is concerned with Antonio and Shylock. Shylock is always talking of his rights. In his case this right takes two forms, the human rights which he, as a Jew, has been denied and the legal rights which he is determined to have.

In the scene in which he agrees to lend the money without any interest, he implies in a highly ironical speech that he has every right to lend the money on account of the way he has been treated:

> Shall I bend low in a bondman's key
> With bated breath and whisper humbleness,
> Say this:
> Fair sir, you spit on me on Wednesday last,
> You spurned me such a day; another time
> You called me dog, and for these courtesies
> I'll lend you thus much moneys?[10]

His consciousness of the right to a respected place in society, which he has been denied, is so acute that it seems to him that he has every right to take revenge, if and when he can.

As the play progresses Shylock's insistence on his legal rights come to the fore. Thus, in the third scene of the third Act, putting Antonio in the prison, he says again and again, "I will have my bond." He speaks only sixteen lines in the scene, and this sentence is repeated five times. When next he appears in the Trial scene, it is to stand upon his rights from the very beginning. This insistence on his rights makes him deaf to all pleas for mercy and turns him into an inhuman monster. Shakespeare shows that extreme insistence on one's rights is bound to lead up to infringement upon other person's rights and may also lead to tragedy. Of course for the exigencies of the plot it can be said that had Shylock been merciful the highly dramatic Trial scene would not have been so dramatic.

The theme of justice is mingled with the theme of rights. Shylock has suffered much injustice on account of being a Jew and this turns his thoughts to revenge. He manages to take his revenge in such a way that his actions become legally justifiable and he can therefore insist on having justice:

> If you deny me, fie upon your law!
> I stand for judgement: answer; shall I have it?[11]

When Portia argues in favour of him it is as an upholder of justice that he praises her. Portia turns the tables on him and insists on his having just justice as he had done a minute earlier:

> For as thou urgest justice, be assured
> Thou shalt have justice, more than thou desirest.[12]

Unfortunately, justice is a two-edged weapon, and it has now turned against him and so he loses everything, even his religion. Shakespeare shows how, taken to its extremes, justice can turn men into inhuman merciless monsters who, through insistence on legal justice, become blind to all considerations of human justice and have to suffer.

In a way, therefore, the themes of right and of justice also point out that extremes should be avoided at all costs. Not only does the exercise of absolute right and justice infringe upon other person's rights but, taken to its extremes, even the concepts of right and justice become ambiguous and can lead to tragedy. More than anything else, even such positive concepts, in extreme cases, can turn men away from humanitarian considerations and moral issues may lose their clear-cut character. These are the truths that touch all men at all times. The critic Ulrici points out:

> Right and wrong become indistinguishable when carried to their utmost limits and are finally merged in the source of all true life—the love and mercy of God.[13]

The Theme of Relation of Man to Property

This is a theme which has been pointed out by G.G. Gervinus and is one of the influential views, for it has been later echoed by others as well:

> The intention of the poet in *The Merchant of Venice* was to depict the relation of man to property.[14]

This is a theme that embraces all the plots in the play—the Antonio-Shylock plot, the Portia-Bassanio plot and the Lorenzo-Jessica plot.

Property can be considered in its many different forms: landed property, merchandise, money. In this, in addition to these, we have another kind of property, for one's own children are also considered as the parent's property. We saw in the second theme we considered how parental rights were exercised by Portia's father. This was possible only because Portia was considered as property.

(i) *The Antonio-Shylock Plot.* Here property is seen at its crudest and most obvious form. Antonio is a wealthy man, for he has many ships with rich merchandise. He, however, is a man who makes good use of his property, for he uses it to stand guarantee for Bassanio. He also lends money to the needy without interest, for which Shylock hates him. Moreover, when borrowers cannot pay back to Shylock, he gives them money, as he himself says:

> I often delivered from his forfeiture
> Many that have at times made moan to me.[15]

When, in the Trial scene, he gets half of Shylock's property, he gives it to Lorenzo very freely. His relationship with his property is a very positive one, and he is rewarded by the dramatist by having his ships back. He is the master of his property, not its slave.

Exactly the opposite is the case with Shylock. His property is hard cash and jewellery. He increases this property by lending money on interest. He finds precedence for this practice in the scriptures. The trouble with him is, his love of money has changed his moral values. This has its serious as well as its comic aspects. The comic aspect is highlighted by the two young men when they talk about his reaction on discovering Jessica's elopement. She has fled with his money, and he does not know which loss to bemoan the more:

> My daughter!—O my ducats!—O my daughter!
> Fled with a Christian!—O my Christian ducats!
> Justice, the law, my ducats and my daughter![16]

This brings us to another kind of property which Shylock has and not Antonio—it is his daughter. He is not a tyrannical father, and depends on her for the safekeeping of his house, and becomes frantic when she deserts him.

Shylock's relationship with his property has bred negative qualities in him and therefore at the end of the play he loses everything. He becomes as nothing when his property is taken away from him.

(ii) *The Portia-Bassanio Plot.* The relationship of man to his property is explored in many ways in this part of the play. The precise nature of Portia's wealth is not made clear. It is very probable that most of her property is landed property, though she has a considerable amount of money also, since she offers three times the money Antonio owes, to Bassanio, on learning of the former's predicament. Her relationship with her property is a positive one, for she freely offers it in order to help others.

There is, however, another aspect of this. Just as Portia is a woman of property so is she, in her turn, the property of her father. He denied her human rights and looked upon her as his own property to be disposed of as he thought fit. Portia accepts this. She tells each of her suitors that she will marry him if he chooses the right casket.

Property, in a symbolic manner, presents another aspect in this plot. In the guise of the caskets, it controls Portia's fate and either guides or misleads the suitors. The gold casket represents gold as the silver casket represents a humbler kind of money. In other words, the caskets challenge the choosers' sense of value and of money.

Bassanio's relationship with money or property is a curious one, for he is a confirmed spendthrift. He has wasted all his property and is already in debt. Shakespeare depicts a young man whose wealth, or lack of it, both sit lightly on him. He is a happy-go-lucky young man for whom property is unearned and a part of life. It is necessary to lead a comfortable life, but it is not life itself. He is rewarded with love as well as money. Acquisition of money does not alter his nature, for he rushes off to rescue Antonio with double the amount due.

There is, however, a certain paradox in the situation. It is ironical that he should reject gold (he rejects the golden casket), for it is the gold borrowed from Shylock that has enabled him to come and court Portia. It is surprising that he does not think of this fact. But his relation to property is a highly positive one and he is rewarded in the end with love as well as property.

(iii) *The Lorenzo-Jessica Plot.* Here is another couple with a very careless and happy-go-lucky attitude to property, just like Bassanio. Lorenzo is deeply in love with Jessica and it is her virtue, wisdom and beauty that matters to him, not the ducats and the jewels she steals from her father. Money hardly ever enters his conversation. We do not know whether he has any private means or not.

All this holds true for Jessica as well. Jessica takes a casket full of gold when she elopes, but she proceeds to get rid of money in a feckless manner during her honeymoon, spending four scores of ducats in one night at Genoa. Shakespeare, looks with indulgence upon the young lovers' cavalier attitude to money and gives them love as well as wealth.

This theme, thus, is to be found in all the three plots. It in turn weaves all these three, acting as the unifying principle. Gervinus has pointed out:

> The question of man's relation to property is ever at the same time a question of his relation to man, as it cannot be imagined apart from man.[17]

The Theme of the Interdependence of Human Beings

This point of view has been explained by Max Plowman:

> The theme of *The Merchant of Venice* is the interdependence of human beings in civilized society—an inviolable interdependence.[18]

This interpretation of the theme is also a very valuable one, for this is a theme that does apply to every character and their relationship. There is, as it were, an unwritten law in society by virtue of which human beings depend upon each other. It is seen at its best in the relationship between Antonio and Bassanio. Right at the outset we come to know that the latter has borrowed money from Antonio and rests secure in the knowledge that, should he need more, he can depend on Antonio, for the bond between them is the bond of selfless love. This dependence is not on Bassanio's part alone, it is reciprocated. When the time comes Bassanio takes twice the amount due and rushes to the rescue of Antonio. In other words, the two of them can depend implicitly on each other.

Another wonderful instance of this interdependence is to be seen in the relationship between Lorenzo and Jessica. She depends on Lorenzo so implicitly that she leaves her father's house and her religion for his sake. Lorenzo's dependence on her is on the same level. It is not for nothing that he takes her for his torch-bearer, for his life will be lit by her.

The same interdependence prevails between Bassanio and Portia. Once the right casket is chosen Portia places herself, heart and soul, in his hands. Bassanio's dependence on her is at oncc apparent, for she has to make good his trust in her which the news about Antonio makes him repose on her.

Indeed, more dependence is placed on Portia than on anyone else for, in the law-court every one, including the duke, depends on her to save Antonio. So does Portia depend on many others to enable her to defend Antonio. She has to depend on Lorenzo to look after her house in her absence. Secondly she has to depend on her servant Balthasar to promptly go to Bellario and get, not only legal advice, but the disguises as well. Next, she has to depend on Bellario to help her out. Finally she depends on Nerissa to accompany her in her adventure and support her.

The network of interdependence is a wide and complex one. Shakespeare shows what happens to those who depend upon each other and value that dependence. As Max Plowman has emphasized:

> All the sympathetic characters are shown as living in happy human interdependence. On them the sun of fortune shines in the end: they come to weal. All who arrogate to themselves wealth or merit come to woe.[19]

The Theme of Usury

This theme has been emphasized by E.C. Pettet. Usury was an important social evil of the time, and Shakespeare gives an extensive treatment of it:

> He seized his opportunity for a full dramatic discussion of the whole subject of usury.[20]

The importance of this theme can hardly be called into question. Usury was a feature of Elizabethan society that could not be neglected. It was a social evil which thrived because of the extravagant and thriftless way of living adopted by the aristocracy. Most of the great lords of the time borrowed money, for they lived beyond their income. Contemporary records show how much certain lords owed to the usurers. Sir Philip Sidney owed six thousand pounds. Shakespeare's own patron, the Earl of Southampton was so heavily in debt that he had to surrender his estates to the creditors and had no place to live in.

In this play we have on one hand the attitude of the Christians to the usurers, which was one of contempt and, on the other hand, the exact opposite of this—a person whose livelihood depends on usury. Antonio tells Shylock that he never takes interest when lending money:

> I neither lend nor borrow
> By taking, nor by giving of excess.[21]

His own attitude, as well as that of Bassanio towards usury is one of contempt. Moneylending with interest had been made legal in England by 1571, but the religious and moral stigma attached to usury was still very strong and many books and pamphlets were written against the practice. It is not that Shakespeare himself did not share this antipathy to usury. It is a known fact that when a friend, Mr. Quyny wanted to borrow twenty-five pounds from him, he at once gave him the amount. The question of charging interest simply did not arise.

Shylock's attitude, on the other hand, is the exact opposite. For him it is a way of earning a living, and, as he thought, even enjoined by the scriptures. The chief reason he hates Antonio is that Antonio not only derides usury but also throws obstacles in his way by lending money gratis. Even worse, when Shylock's debtors cannot pay him back and go to Antonio for help, he helps them to avoid forfeiture.

Because of this basic difference in attitude, there is a difference in the use of language also. Many words bear a different denotation to Shylock—different from those they bear to Christians. Thus when Bassanio approaches him and tells him that Antonio will stand guarantee, then Shylock says "Antonio is a good man," and on Bassanio's taking umbrage, explains it:

> my meaning, in saying he is a good man is to have you understand me, that he is sufficient.[22]

Bassanio is the typical, feckless young man-about-town on whom usury thrived. Extravagant and careless, men like him lost their property, mortgaging them to moneylenders.

The play shows how moneylending and borrowing can ruin men, but it also shows that love and friendship may stave off that ruin, and create happiness by banishing it. In the end it is the usurer who is defeated and his money goes to exactly the kind of person to whom he used to lend it: the careless and thriftless young Christian lover Lorenzo. The practice of usury also distorts a man's ethical outlook, so that "good" comes to mean a man of substance, not a man of integrity.

The Theme of Justice and Mercy

This theme has been put forward by two very important authorities on Elizabethan drama, Nevill Coghill and M.C. Bradbrook:

> [...] the theme of this play; which is very plainly set forth as Justice and Mercy; the law and the love that is the fulfilling of that law, the gold of Venice and the gold of Belmont.[23]

This theory sees the entire play as a contrast between law and love, or, as Bradbrook puts it, the gold of Venice and the gold of Belmont. On one hand there is Shylock who stands for law and on the other there is Portia who stands for Mercy. Shylock insistence on the legal validity of his bond occurs throughout the play. "Let him look to his bond" and "I will have my bond" are repeated countless times. In the Trial scene he insists upon having justice and law in almost every second sentence he speaks. Unfortunately the very law he stands for is turned against him, and he has to acquiesce, willy-nilly. As Portia puts it, he shall have both Justice and law:

As thou urgest justice, be assured
Thou shalt have justice, more than thou desirest.[24]

Portia, on the other hand, stands for Mercy. Not only does she go to save Antonio out of pure, disinterested philanthropy but it is she who delivers the famous mercy-speech. Later, when Shylock proves to be beyond all such appeals, she stands for the terrible figure of Justice, meted out to Shylock for his lack of human charity. Though Bassanio offers the money, she does not let Shylock have it. Before and after this transformation, however, she stands for love and romance, against which the world of commerce is pitted. It is the spirit of romance that triumphs in the end:

> The contrast between Justice and Mercy, embodied in figures of so winning a grace that the critics talk of them as if they lived.[25]

The Theme of Love's Wealth

The fact that love is the theme of all romantic comedies is well-known and generally accepted. Within this, however, there are many variations. One such variation has been presented by John Russell Brown according to whom Shakespeare explores the theme of love's wealth in these comedies:

> Of all the comedies *The Merchant of Venice* is the most completely informed by Shakespeare's idea of love's wealth.[26]

According to this view love's true wealth, as seen by Shakespeare, is in giving and not gaining, it is cherished in bounty. Love has its own value which is totally different from commercial value which is measured in gold. It can be seen in forms as different as the three different stories that make up the play.

In the Antonio-Shylock plot the friendship between Antonio and Bassanio present love's wealth. This friendship is an all-comprehensive friendship that is ready to sacrifice all. Antonio is offering everything to Bassanio. He has but one condition, honour:

And if it stand, as you yourself still do
Within the eye of honour, be assur'd

My purse, my person, my extremest means
Lie all unlock'd to your occasions.[27]

It is the wealth of unfathomable love that is presented to Bassanio, whose commercial value is as nothing. Bassanio, too, reciprocates this love, for "love is repaid by love alone." When he gets the fateful letter in the casket scene he cries out:

Here is a letter, lady
The paper is as the body of my friend
And every word in it a gaping wound
Issuing life-blood.[28]

In his farewell speech Antonio presents his love as being valued far higher than life itself. Nor is Bassanio behindhand when he says that he is ready to place life itself and everything else in Shylock's hands if he could but save his friend. These are no empty words. If, as John Russell Brown says, love is presented in this play as a commodity that can be bought and sold, these two are ready to pay the highest price for it.

The story of the caskets is the first instance taken by Brown to illustrate his theory about love's wealth. Each of the caskets pose a challenge and the chooser is served accordingly. The leaden casket reads "who chooseth me must give and hazard all he hath." This is what Bassanio is ready to do and therefore he gets Portia. In the Trial scene Bassanio once more proves that he is truly ready to give and hazard all he has for love.

Portia, also, is rich in the wealth of love. Indeed she is fortune's darling, for she has worldly wealth as well as the wealth of love. When facing a challenge, she rises superbly to the occasion, telling Bassanio that he can take a virtually unlimited amount of money to rescue his friend. But, then, she knows that love cannot be measured with worldly goods and so, to make assurance doubly sure, she herself goes to Venice. It is out of pure, disinterested friendly love that she acts as she does. She is rewarded with all that a woman can desire—worldly wealth, love and friendship.

Lorenzo and Jessica also, hazard everything for love. They too are rich in love's wealth. It is seen in the last scene of the play how those who can risk everything for love get everything they desire. For the three pairs of lovers, love is something more valuable than all commercial gains. As Brown observes:

> If *Merchant of Venice* is seen as a play about Shakespeare's idea of love's wealth, this last Act is a fitting sequel to the discord of the trial scene.[29]

The Theme of Loneliness

This is an extraordinary view of the play. It is presented by Graham Midgeley who neglects the romantic interest. He thinks that the two plots of Portia and Bassanio, and Lorenzo and Jessica are largely side-issues, and the real focus of interest is Antonio and, along with him, Shylock:

> I would suggest that the two focal points of the play are Shylock, and, not the lovers or the romantic theme, but Antonio [...]. The play is, in effect, a twin study in loneliness.[30]

One of the most eminent critics of Shakespearean comedy, H.B. Charlton, had said very much the same thing. He, too, had more or less disregarded the theme of love and concentrated his interest on Shylock. Graham Midgeley is of the opinion that the play should not be considered as a romantic comedy. Shakespeare himself, by naming the play after Antonio meant it to have a different slant—one towards Antonio and not towards the love theme.

According to his view both Antonio and Shylock are lonely men and it is their loneliness that has been emphasized repeatedly in the play. Antonio's great friend Bassanio is not content with the friendship of Antonio, and, in a word, betrays Antonio by wanting to marry. This is the reason why Antonio, in the first scene, is sad. He does not know the reason for his sadness, for even to himself he cannot admit the fact that he is sad at Bassanio's desertion. It is significant that at the end of the play everyone is paired off and Antonio is left alone. This rarely happens in romantic comedy. Moreover, in the original story Antonio's counterpart, Ansaldo, is also married off, but here, most significantly, Shakespeare has departed from the source.

Shylock, also, presents a pathetic picture for he is betrayed by his daughter. Right in the beginning of the play his servant

Launcelot Gobbo leaves his service and then Jessica too leaves him. In fact he loses everything: his money, his daughter, his religion. Who can be more lonely than Shylock? He is simply dropped out of the play after the Trial scene. Antonio is at least present on the stage in the last scene as a valued friend, but Shylock, as it were, ceases to exist. The two characters are widely different from each other, but, as Graham Midgeley points out:

> For all these differences, there is the basic kinship in the Jew and the Merchant, the kinship of loneliness.[31]

Besides these, certain other themes have been suggested for *The Merchant,* but most of them are variations on the theme of love. All of Shakespeare's plays have so much complexity that they reward repeated readings and on each reading different considerations come to the reader's mind. There is such wonderful flexibility in his plays that they can be made to fit almost any interpretation, which is further proof of their universal quality.

REFERENCES

1. Charlton, H.B., *Shakespearian Comedy,* Methuen & Co. Ltd., University Pbk. ed., no date. 21.
2. *Ibid.*
3. *The Merchant of Venice,* Act I, scene i, ll. 162-69.
4. Act III, sc. ii, ll. 61-62.
5. Act III, sc. ii, ll. 108-14.
6. Act II, sc. vi, ll. 53-57.
7. Act III, sc. ii, ll. 198-208.
8. Wilders, J., ed. *Shakespeare: The Merchant of Venice.* Macmillan student edition. Casebook series. London. 1970: 32.
9. *The Merchant,* Act I, sc. ii, ll. 22-24.
10. Act I, sc. iii, ll. 122-28.
11. Act IV, sc. i, ll. 101-03.
12. Act IV, sc. i, ll. 315-16.
13. Wilders, J., *op. cit.,* 33.
14. *Ibid.,* 34.
15. Act III, sc. iii, ll. 22-24.
16. Act II, sc. viii, ll. 14-16.
17. Wilders, J., *op. cit.,* 35.
18. *Ibid.,* 80.

19. *Ibid.*
20. *Ibid.*, 100.
21. Act I, sc. iii, ll. 60-61.
22. Act I, sc. iii, ll. 14-16.
23. Wilders, J., *op. cit.*, 133.
24. Act IV, sc. i., ll. 315-16.
25. Wilders, J., *op. cit.*, 141.
26. *Ibid.*, 163.
27. Act II, sc. i, ll. 136-39.
28. Act III, sc. ii, ll. 262-65.
29. Wilders, J., *op. cit.*, 170.
30. *Ibid.*, 195.
31. *Ibid.*, 204.

5

ART OF CHARACTERIZATION

A dramatic character is different from a character in real life, yet it has to be realistic. It is an artistic representation of a human being in a play, on the stage, and as such takes on a distinctive meaning of its own. All the Elizabethan dramatists Shakespeare included, followed the classical theory of characters current at the time and each, with his own individual talent and artistry, presented characters which caught and held the attention of the audience. The same material was available to all, but Shakespeare created wonderful characters which no other dramatist could. It is here that the quality of his art of characterization deserves special attention, for one of the many reasons for his supremacy over the other play wrights of his time is the excellence of his characters. Certain basic facts in this connection are:

(1) His characters are well-rounded, individual beings.

(2) In addition to individuality some characters have universal dimensions.

(3) In addition to individuality and universality, some characters rise to archetypal, mythical proportions.

(4) Some of his characters are such that they have become part and parcel of the great gallery of English dramatic characters—immortal portrayals.

(5) He has given more such characters to the gallery of dramatic characters than any other writers.

(6) Even his minor characters are not neglected. When they come on the stage, for however short a time, they come alive and gain individuality.

(7) The range of his characters is immense. No other English dramatist can boast of having covered as wide a section of humanity as he has.

(8) Even just one of the features given above is enough for a dramatist to have gained immortality and in Shakespeare we have a combination of all. The characters of *The Merchant* display all these qualities.

His readers recognised the importance of his characters and his mastery over the art of delineating them quite early. One of the earliest critics, G.G. Gervinus has remarked:

> That which most distinguishes him and his poetry, that in which he maintains his freest motion, that from which he designs the structure of his pieces and events, creating the given substance anew, is ever the characters themselves and the motives of their actions.[1]

As his mastery over the art of writing plays developed, Shakespeare's art of characterization also developed. Drama, as Cicero had said, is "imitation of life, image of truth, mirror of customs," and life is made of men and women, that is to say, characters. Delineation of characters therefore, carries great importance in drama and Aristotle accords characters the second place—second only to plot. It is the measure of Shakespeare's greatness that there is continuous development in his depiction of humanity. There is a well-marked and strong line of progression in this respect in all the four stages of his career.

In the first phase of his career Shakespeare had not yet mastered his art. This was the time of apprenticeship. The characters of this time are not very well-developed. There are signs of immaturity in the presentation of human nature. It is difficult, for example, to differentiate between the king and his lords in *Love's Labour's Lost*, as it is difficult to differentiate among the Princess's ladies. Lord Berowne and Lady Rosalind, of course, stand out because of their wittiness, but there is little to choose among the other characters. The same is the case between the two pairs of lovers in *A Midsummer Night's Dream*. As a matter of fact the only memorable character of this time does not come from the aristocracy but from the lower classes. Bottom of *A Midsummer Night's Dream* has gained immortality as the only representative of solid, down-to-earth common sense in the entire play. The seeds of later development, however, can already be seen in these plays. He has already started to endow some of his characters with individuality. Puck in *A Midsummer*, and Bottom, for example, have been given distinct individual qualities and Richard III is a highly individual character. They are remembered even after the play is over.

By the time that he reached the second stage of his career Shakespeare had attained mastery over his craft and in each play we have, not only highly credible, realistic human beings, but characters that have become definite contributions to English drama, enhancing our understanding of human nature. It is true that at this time Shakespeare has not yet become pre-occupied with evil and negative characters, but his understanding of human nature is already surprising. The ability to plumb the depths of the inmost nature of man and woman has already developed. Not only does he give portrayals of important male characters (Shylock is but one of them), but of unforgettable women as well. It has to be noted that his most vital and captivating heroines (Portia is but one of them) come from the plays of this period. They overshadow the male characters.

Yet this is not the peak of his achievement, for the great tragic characters belong to the third phase of his career. The plays of this phase show deep insight into the less attractive aspects of human mind. Emotions like hatred, jealousy, greed for power are all seen in the bright light of a detached understanding. Yet this understanding is not inhumanly detached—it is full of pity and is not censorious, that is why we have tragedy, evoking pity and terror, and not satirical comedy as Ben Jonson produced. Shakespeare had too much sympathy for the human animal and could not hold him up to ridicule.

It would seem difficult to progress beyond this state, but the last plays of Shakespeare can show further development. Now we have characters who can hardly be judged according to ordinary social standards, for they gain a nearly religious significance. The main characters are sinners but they are purified through repentance and on the other hand there are the heroines who are symbols of purity and innocence.

In order to fully understand the main features of Shakespeare's art of characterization (not only in *The Merchant* but in the other plays as well) it is necessary to know a few basic theories of characters current in his own time with which he must have been familiar. Aristotle had laid down certain specific rules for characters in drama and besides these there were the conventions filtered through the blood-and-thunder tragedies of Seneca. More important even than these, there were the "characters" of Theophrastus made familiar through translations and books like Sir Thomas Overbury's *Characters* and Newton's *Touchstone of Complexions.* Hall's *Characters of Virtues and Vices* was another such work which presented a rich portrait-gallery for dramatists. These books gave definitions and explanations of many different kinds of characters and were, therefore, a blessing to all dramatists. Shakespeare, with such conventional lists ready at hand, could use them as foundation and build his own superstructure over them. On one hand he had the theory of how to create characters and on the other he had these set characters as examples. He put his own observation of human nature in general and of individuals in particular in conjunction with these and produced his immortal characters, whose range and variety show the extent of his observations.

The theory about dramatic characters which had helped him as well as the other dramatists of his age goes back to Aristotle. This is rather unexpected for Aristotle had dealt with tragedy in detail but he had not said much about comedy. In his *Poetics* he has given a definition of comedy and said that he will deal with this subject later. The definition he gave is:

> Comedy is, as we have said, an imitation of characters of a low type—not however, in the full scene of the word bad, the Ludicrous being merely a subdivision of the ugly. It consists in some defect or ugliness which is not painful or destructive.[2]

Here, therefore, the characters are of prime importance. Aristotle does not say anything about the plot, style or any other feature of comedy in this definition. We come to know that comic characters are inferior to the average characters. This inferiority does not have anything truly bad or evil in it. It is such a defect in the character as provokes laughter in the audience. It can be a physical defect or a mental one as well. Later in the course of *Poetics* he gives certain attributes of dramatic characters. It is not that he talks specially of tragic characters or of comic characters. These rules apply to any kind of dramatic characters.

He defines a character by laying emphasis on the qualities inherent in them, the qualities which differentiate or motivate their actions. Since these qualities, therefore, are of prime importance, it is necessary to know what they are. It should be remembered that he does not mean individual qualities here, but more general qualities. According to him there are four main attributes that dramatic characters should have:

(1) Proportion
(2) Appropriateness
(3) Realism and
(4) Consistency.

The first quality, Proportion, is also known as "goodness." The character should speak or act in such a way that a moral purpose should be clearly conveyed. When the moral purpose is good the character, also, is good. Thus when Antonio agrees to lend Bassanio the money to go to Belmont by signing a bond that puts his own life in peril, the moral purpose is unquestionably good. Moreover, it should also be remembered that he quite strongly declares that "honour" is important to him. Whatever Bassanio is going to do with the money thus gained, honour should not be jeopardised:

> I pray you, good Bassanio, let me know it,
> And if it stand, as you yourself still do,
> Within the eye of honour, be assur'd,
> My purse, my person, my extremest means,
> Lie all unlock'd to your occasion.[3]

This concept of moral goodness, moreover, varies with each character. Refraining from theft will be regarded as a good quality in, for example, a servant like Launcelot Gobbo, but it is taken for granted in a gentleman and will not be regarded as a virtue in such a case. Shakespeare's characters have this quality in the right degree. He gives good as well as bad traits in the right proportions to each of his creations. Evil characters like Iago in *Othello*, Iachimo in *Cymbeline* are villains and therefore they have little that is good in them. His great artistry is to be seen in the tragic heroes in whom good and evil are so admirably balanced that we admire as well as pity them. He has, of course, excelled himself in Shylock whom, in spite of everything, we come to pity in the end. Not only does this character rise to symbolic heights in the terrible speech "Hath not a Jew eyes," but at the end of the trial he is deprived of everything that makes life worth living. One has to concede the justice of his complaint when he bursts out:

> Nay, take my life, and all; pardon not that:
> You take my house, when you do take the prop
> That doth sustain my house; you do take my life
> When you do take the means whereby I live.[4]

Here one also remembers how he is a bereaved father, whose only child has disgracefully deserted him. Thus Shakespeare portrays a characters who is not all evil, who evokes our sympathy. Shakespeare does not call attention to any good quality he may have—he does far more, he makes Shylock human. No mere Aristotelian rules of proportion etc., can explain this, it goes far beyond that.

Appropriateness, the second quality given by Aristotle, signifies that each character will have to be given attributes that are proper to him. A courtier should be elegant and polished and all the courtiers, for example, in *Love's Labour's Lost* are like that. An heiress should, because she comes from an affluent family, be full of social graces and elegant, and Portia is both. She is also a romantic heroine and as such has to be witty and attractive in order to be able to capture the heart of Bassanio. Accordingly Shakespeare endows her with all these qualities that are appropriate to her position in life and in society. The fact that she is much more than all these things put together is due to the individual artistry of Shakespeare.

In the context of Appropriateness, Aristotle had given an example by pointing out that manly valour is inappropriate in a woman. Thus when, Viola, the heroine of *Twelfth Night,* is disguised as a page-boy, she is afraid when she is made to fight Sir Andrew Aguecheek and we have occasion for laughter as well as dramatic irony. The characters in *The Merchant* have the qualities that are appropriate to them. Shylock, a usurer, wants to increase his wealth which is quite appropriate for him, but then Shakespeare has given him a speech which, while perfectly appropriate for a persecuted Jew, at the same time gains the sympathy of the reader.

Realism is the third quality Aristotle wants in a dramatic character. A character should be true to life. This might seem to be an obvious quality but in the hands of inferior dramatists a character might easily become unrealistic. No character of Shakespeare is unrealistic. They are such characters as can be found in real life, under ordinary circumstances. This quality of realism is particularly relevant as far as comedy is concerned, for in tragedy the audience sees kings and heroes, who are not like simple, average men. Here there are many varieties of realism, for a character can be (a) slightly better than the average man (b) just like the average man (c) a little inferior to the average man. We find all of these kinds in our dramatist. No one ever feels that a character of Shakespeare is utterly unrealistic, though one might feel that certain traits in some of them are a little exaggerated. All Jews may not be like Shylock, all kings may not be like King Lear, all jealous husbands may not kill their wives as Othello does, but one always feels that his characters reflect real human beings. It is particularly in the minor characters that the quality of realism is seen at its most effective. In *Merchant of Venice* the two young Venetians, Solanio and Salarino, are careless, happy-go-lucky young men. They are ready to help Lorenzo in eloping with Jessica, take Antonio's letter to Bassanio, and have a little fun by baiting the dog Jew. Had any of them suddenly become sympathetic to Shylock, or advised Lorenzo against eloping with Jessica, that would not have been realistic. Shylock's scapegrace servant Launcelot Gobbo is a clownish low class Christian and leaves his service for hope of better rewards. This, too, is perfectly realistic. On the other hand one remembers Adam, the old servant of Orlando in *As You Like It*, who accompanies his young master to the forest. But, then, he is a family retainer, had brought up Orlando, like a son, right from childhood. Feudal loyalty is in his very marrow-bone. When he goes with Orlando, it is perfectly realistic. It speaks volumes for Shakespeare's own knowledge of human nature that even in utterly minor characters like servants he can create such diametrically opposing characters as Adam and Launcelot, yet make them thoroughly realistic.

Another such minor character in *The Merchant* is Tubal. He is designated as Shylock's friend and comes only once on the stage, in the first scene of the third Act. He had been sent to gather any information he could about Jessica. Now he comes to give the news. He has good news as well as bad news and being Shylock's friend wants to spare him the agony as much as possible. So he tries to lift up Shylock's spirits again and again by telling him about Antonio's misfortunes. This is quite realistic, though this scene has been looked upon as a comic one, mainly because of Shylock's varying reactions on hearing the different items of news, alternately, about his daughter and Antonio.

Consistency has been listed by Aristotle as the last of the four qualities, but it is, perhaps, more important than the others. A character must be consistent from the beginning to the end. Shylock must not suddenly change into a generous character like Antonio. Portia should not turn into a dull, humourless woman, Gratiano must not suddenly become a sombre and melancholy person. We might ask: but in real life people change. Should not such changes be presented in the stage? The answer is: such changes do take place and should be presented on the stage in a fully convincing and credible manner. Othello changes from an ardent lover into a murderously jealous man in front of our eyes but Shakespeare makes it perfectly believable. There is change and development in each of the characters, but these changes are presented in so realistic a manner that they never seem to be inconsistent with the basic nature of the character and herein lies the artistry of Shakespeare.

Moreover, another feature has to be taken into consideration. It must be remembered that Aristotle was writing with the other rules of drama in the background of his mind. The rule of the unity of time is in question. It was taken for granted at that time that the actual story told by the dramatist should cover, at the maximum, a full day, and no more. Aristotle could not imagine that the one and the same play could cover, as in the case of *The Merchant,* at least three months, or more than sixteen years, as in the case of *The Winter's Tale.* In human life, time is an all-important factor. A man may change radically over the years and in such cases such changes cannot be called inconsistent. King Leontes, in the beginning of *The Winter's Tale,* is so jealous that he wants to kill his friend. Then no less than sixteen years pass, and we see him as a thoroughly changed, penitent man at the end. Such a change is quite consistent. *The Merchant,* however, does not cover such a long expanse of time, and, within the time-span involved (slightly more than three months) the characters remain consistent with their nature.

Apart from these rules, there were concrete examples in front of Shakespeare. There were certain "set characters" handed down by the classical scholars. In comedy, for example, three varieties of characters could be portrayed: (a) the buffoon (b) the ironic (c) the impostor. These characters, however, are meant for satiric comedies of the kind that Ben Jonson wrote, not for the romantic comedies of Shakespeare. Aristotle himself had given the definition and description of six more characters to be used in drama. After this the commentators on Aristotle went on adding to the list, and finally Theophrastus gave about a hundred "set characters," defining, naming and describing them. These "set characters," were, it must be remembered, available to every dramatist of the time, but Shakespeare created a number of unforgettable, immortal characters that others could not. It is here that his originality and capacity makes his supremacy shine forth. He was not limited by these characters available to him, but:

> While keeping to the old principles that comedy portrays characters he profoundly modified it by deepening and strengthening each separate character and developing the relations between different characters.[5]

In these golden comedies, therefore, we find Shakespeare's art of characterization at its maturest, when each character is life-like, and perfectly proportioned. They are highly individualistic yet universal. Highlighting this aspect, M.C. Bradbrook has further remarked:

> It is the peculiar virtue of this play [...] that the characters are at the same time fully human and symbolic or larger than human.[6]

This is another aspect of Shakespeare's art of characterization—the symbolic depth he gives to his characters. There is no provision for this in classical theories. Aristotle provides for such characters as are better than the average, like the average, and worse than the average. In every instance, however, he insists on realism. The concept of symbolic or allegorical characters does not tally with these ideas. Shakespeare, however, had the solid foundation of the mediaeval morality plays with their allegorical characters to support his own imagination. Many of his characters therefore, gain a symbolic depth, like King Lear, Miranda, Shylock and others. This achievement is all the more miraculous when it is taken into consideration that he does this while fully observing the rules and conventions of his time. Shylock's character is quite in accordance with the contemporary conventional attitude towards a Jew, and at the same time he becomes symbolic of oppressed and persecuted humanity.

Within the limited scope of romantic comedies Shakespeare has given a wide range of characters—from the romantic lovers to the vengeful Jew, from the devoted friend to the comic servant. These characters are in keeping with the rules governing dramatic characters, yet well-rounded individuals.

REFERENCES

1. Wilders, J., *op. cit.*, 34.
2. Butcher, S.L., transl., *Aristotle's Theory of Poetry and Fine Arts*, New Delhi, Kalyani Pubs., 1981, 21.
3. *The Merchant*, Act, I, sc. i, ll. 135-39.
4. Act IV, sc. i, ll. 374-77.
5. Bradbrook, M.C., *The Growth and Structure of Elizabethan Comedy*, Cambridge, 1954, 76.
6. Wilders, J., *op. cit.*, 134.

6

THE MAJOR CHARACTERS

There are several important characters in our play, the most important of whom are Portia and Shylock. Next in importance are Antonio and Bassanio. Each of these, while conforming to the type expected by Elizabethan audience is also a fully-rounded individual and at times, especially in the case of Shylock, going several steps beyond mere individuality to gain universal dimensions. Portia and Shylock, specially, have been analysed and interpreted in a number of ways by various critics. One should remember that, in whatever way the character might be interpreted, no one view can be taken to be the last word on the subject.

Portia

Shakespeare's heroines are a class by themselves, and the four heroines of his golden comedies form a group of their own: Portia, Viola, Rosalind and Beatrice. To these, in respect of wit, may be added Rosalind of *Love's Labour's Lost.* All of these four heroines are witty, lively, and resourceful. Three of them, Portia, Viola and Rosalind adopt disguises. Out of these four, Portia is not as witty as Rosalind or Beatrice, nor is she as sober and grave as Viola. She strikes a mean between these two, being witty and light-hearted, but having the sobriety and judgement in her which will justify her ability to disguise herself as a lawyer and win a difficult case.

Her physical beauty is but a pointer to the beauty of her personality. She, along with the other heroines of these comedies, as Granville-Barker puts it "embodied an ideal lodged for long in Shakespeare's imagination." This physical beauty is the first thing that overwhelms the young romantic lover, Bassanio, but virtue and beauty are valued equally by him. Portia, in fact, has every thing,—wealth, beauty and virtue-listed in that order by Bassanio. Granville-Barker also pointed out how there is a dichotomy in these heroines who adopt a disguise. On one hand there is the suggestion of utter femininity and virgin innocence and on the other hand there is the disguise of a page-boy. In the case of Portia there is the wise doctor-of-law disguise. The difference between Portia and the boy-Portia is far wider than the difference between Rosalind and Ganymede or between Viola and Cesario. Yet, according to Granville-Barker, this dichotomy is not as sharp as that in the other heroines for Shakespeare presents us with several aspects of Portia, each different from the other so that it is not difficult for us to reconcile the rich lady of Belmont with the doctor of law at the court. There are, as he enumerates, "the heiress and great lady of Belmont," "a mere child," "Portia of resource and command," "school girl laughing with Nerissa." All these, like the lawyer, are but different aspects of this fascinating character:

> Know them all for one Portia, a wise and gallant spirit so virginally enshrined.[1]

The Elizabethans enjoyed what Barker calls the process of the "double negative." It is actually a boy-actor who has dressed up as a girl and when the female character disguises herself as a boy it is, for the audience, a boy dressed as a girl dressed as a boy. This process is not available to us for with us it is a mature actress who presents the character on the stage. Thus, much of the irony of the disguise is lost to us. There are, in spite of this defect, several important aspects of this disguise. One of these aspects is the fact that very often some contingency forces them to adopt a disguise. Rosalind, Viola and Imogen adopt it as a measure of safety. In *The Merchant* itself Jessica dons the dress of a boy in order to make her elopement easy and Nerissa does so at the express wish of her mistress. Their disguises, in other words, serve some personal end. Portia's disguise, however, is not due to any such personal considerations. It is to save Antonio that she disguises herself. In her case it is not any contingency but pure altruism that leads to disguise.

Shakespeare portrays her as a girl who is like a prize in a lottery—whoever chooses the right casket will have her. She cannot refuse to marry such a man even if she dislikes him. Shakespeare takes care to point this out at the outset:

> I may neither choose whom I would, nor refuse whom I dislike, so is the will of a daughter curbed by the will of a dead father.[2]

Yet her sense of honour is keen and not only does she gracefully accept the will of her father, but, when the crucial moment comes, refrains from guiding Bassanio in choosing. Shakespeare, however, was so great an artist that he knew better than to make her a girl of inhuman rectitude and in the fancy song she gives Bassanio a hint by making use of words that rhyme with "lead."

It is in the Trial scene that the full force of her personality is revealed. There is the famous mercy-speech that has the softness of a woman's heart. When this fails she is transformed into the impersonal figure of Justice and condemns Shylock. Bassanio offers three times the principal amount. Portia stops him:

> The Jew shall have all justice;—soft!—no haste:—
> He shall have nothing but the penalty.[3]

A little later, when Shylock, thankful, enough to get his principal, asks for it and Bassanio offers the money, she stops him:

> He hath refused it in the open court
> He shall have merely justice, and the bond.[4]

And then she tightens the screw by quoting the ancient law of Venice which puts Shylock at the mercy of his enemy. This is no soft-hearted woman but the very symbol of justice.

One wonders at the self-possession of this young girl, and the manner in which she conducts the case. She has, one is to suppose, led a cloistered life up till now at Belmont. She has not even met her cousin Dr. Bellario, to tell about legal proceeding for she got the advice about the cases in a letter yet she behaves like a veteran lawyer. Shakespeare has definitely endowed her with much more than ordinary resourcefulness and presence of mind. There is, however, no time to have such thoughts while the play is being enacted on the stage. The turns and twists of the case, the reactions of the others, do not allow us to have any doubtful thoughts. It is only later, if at all, that we wonder at Portia's sagacity. In other words, here we have an instance of what Coleridge calls "willing suspension of disbelief."

Withal, however, she is the heroine of a romantic comedy and the play has to end in accordance with the demands of such plays. So Shakespeare brings her back to the enchanted night at Belmont and gives us the light-hearted ring-episode so that once more the attractive, witty and rich lady of Belmont is reinstated and the play ends with merriment.

Portia's character has been interpreted in many different ways by Shakespeare's readers down the ages. Almost every critic looks at her from a very positive standpoint. She symbolizes youth, beauty and wit to some critics, and to some she symbolizes love's wealth. Thus, pointing to the fact that Bassanio mentions wealth, beauty and virtue, John Russell Brown opines:

> All these comprise her wealth in love.[5]

Not all interpretations are favourable. Harold C. Goddard views her unsympathetically and, analyzing her actions, lays particular stress on the fact that she herself does not show any mercy to Shylock. She speaks eloquently about mercy, but shows herself devoid of it when the time comes:

> The words on mercy are good sentences, well-pronounced [...]. But for Portia they remain just words in the sense that they did not teach her to do the deeds of mercy.[6]

Another point that goes against her is that she causes needless misery and tension to everyone in the Trial scene. She knew, nobody better, the legal quibble that will save Antonio. Why then does she allow the trial to go on for as long as she does? To ask these questions is to treat her just like a real human being, forgetting that she is a dramatic character. After all Shakespeare had to write a Trial scene which should rivet the attention of the audience. The scene is not only the star scene of this play, but one of the most famous scenes in Shakespeare's entire work. All this would have been lost if Portia had finished the case within a few minutes of her arrival. Her conduct in prolonging the scene is in accordance with dramatic needs. But, again, the fact that such an objection should be raised means that the critic is looking at her as a human being, not as an artistic creation. This speaks most effectively about the lifelike, realistic quality of Portia.

Shylock

Shylock is the most controversial character in *The Merchant* and more has been written about him than any other character in it. He is not just a vengeful Jew, but, as the play progresses, comes to represent this oppressed and persecuted race. At the end he gains the reader's sympathy even more because he loses everything, his wealth, his daughter and his religion. Perhaps an Elizabethan audience might have thought this punishment well-deserved, but it will look like cruelty to a modern audience. It is an undeniable fact that Shylock is the only male character who is remembered most vividly even after the play is over.

In the beginning Shylock seems to be quite true to type, like a "set character" presented by Hall or Overbury—a greedy usurer and a hypocrite to boot. Both of these characteristics are conveyed in one and the same speech which is an aside spoken when Bassanio approaches him for the loan:

> I hate him for he is a Christian
> But more for that in low simplicity
> He lends out money gratis and brings down
> The rate of usance here for us in Venice
> If I can catch him once upon the hip
> I will feed fat the ancient grudge I bear him.[7]

As the plot unfolds different aspects of his personality are revealed. We marvel at his sly ingenuity and knowledge of human nature when he persuades Antonio to sign the bond by telling him that it is but a simple joke—it is a "merry sport," "a merry bond." He knows that Antonio's noble nature cannot refuse the hand of friendship he is pretending to extend. His own nature is the total opposite of this, but he knows what Antonio's nature is like and this knowledge carries the highly dubious proposal through.

We see him next when he leaves his house to go to the supper-party being given by Bassanio. He reveals himself as a dictatorial father, forbidding Jessica even to go near the windows to see the masque that might pass along the street.

So far there is nothing to arouse our sympathy or any kind of regard for him. Next, the two young men Salarino and Solanio describe his behaviour at the discovery of Jessica's flight. He is almost crazed with grief, but he is portrayed as a person whose grief, instead of rousing sympathy, provokes laughter, for he laments for his daughter and his money in the same breath, so much so that the entire effect becomes ludicrous.

> My daughter!—O my ducats!—O my daughter!
> Fled with a Christian!—O my Christian ducats!
> Justice! the law! my ducats and my daughter![8]

Here he is a clownish character, but this is a description given by such men as hold him in contempt. The case becomes very different when we see him face to face. The same two young men are there and Shylock delivers a unique speech, one that at once appeals to the audience:

> I am a Jew. Hath not a Jew eyes? Hath not a Jew hands, organs, dimensions, senses, affections, passions? Fed with the same food, hurt with the same weapons, subject to the same diseases, healed by the same means, warmed and cooled by the same winter and summer, as a Christian is? If you prick us, do we not bleed? If you tickle us, do we not laugh? If you poison us, do we not die? and, if you wrong us, shall we not revenge?[9]

Here Shylock is not just Shylock, a Jew, for he has gained symbolic heights, he is the representative of an entire race of Jews who have been persecuted for millennia. It is not only Christians who have persecuted them for they were slaves under the Egyptian rulers even before the coming of Moses. Such a speech, again, has become specially significant for modern readers who have the knowledge of Hitlerian atrocities perpetrated on them just a few decades ago. It is with this feature in mind that M.C. Bradbrook has remarked that in this play:

> The characters are at the same time fully human and symbolic or larger than human.[10]

Such heights, however, are difficult to maintain and it is not necessary for the play either. In fact, if Shakespeare had retained this particular feature from this point onwards then it would not have been in keeping with the story, or, indeed, with the spirit of romantic comedy either. So we see a different aspect of the character when Tubal enters. Once more the clownish aspect is highlighted, for he talks alternately about his ducats, his daughter and Antonio's misfortunes. This, of course, is in accordance with the news he receives from Tubal, but the effect is comic all the same.

Then the villain surfaces again in the Trial scene. Here once again, Shylock is a vengeful Jew, insisting on the letter of the bond and thoroughly uncompromising. It was he himself who had said that the bond was written in sporting spirit. Yet now, this very sporting spirit is thoroughly neglected and he insists on the letter of the law. Appeals to his good nature go unheard. Not only is he not ready to take thrice the amount owing to him, but he is also not ready to arrange for a surgeon. This, on top of all that has gone before, alienates the audience or the reader, and Shylock is looked upon as a monster of cruelty. When the turning-point comes the reader, like Gratiano, rejoices.

His punishment, however, seems to be too severe to a modern reader, for his triple loss—his wealth, his daughter, and his religion—deprives him of everything that makes life worth living. Shakespeare puts a mantle of dignity on him at the moment of defeat. He does not rant or rail. He does not plead for mercy. He does not say, even in an aside, that this is just the kind of treatment he expects from Christians. Instead he merely says:

> I pray you, give me leave to go from hence.
> I am not well. Send the deed after me.
> And I will sign it.[11]

Then he goes out, not to be seen again. The play is a romantic comedy, but it is a tragedy for Shylock who loses everything.

The character of Shylock, thus, undergoes several changes in the play and we might say that Aristotle's rule of consistency has not been observed. This would be a misunderstanding, for Shylock's speeches and actions, though they reveal different aspects of his nature are, nevertheless, quite in keeping with his personality. Aristotle had said elsewhere that changes in a character depend upon circumstances. From this point of view we have a realistic portrayal, for different circumstances do bring out different aspects of a man's personality in real life.

It is, however, undeniable that Shylock's character is not only unique, not only does it offer great opportunities to the actor, but it has attracted more analysis and comments than any other character in this play. Indeed, so striking is his character that in one of the earliest comments on the play, *The Merchant* has been called a tragedy, purely on the strength of this one character. Again, there is the famous story told by Heine:

> There stood behind me in the box a pale British beauty who, at the end of the fourth Act, wept passionately, and many times cried out, "The poor man is wronged."[12]

These are early views. Ever since then numerous interpretations of this character have come up. These interpretations are mostly by literary critics, but actors also have presented this character in many different ways on the stage. At first, that is, in Shakespeare's own time, he was presented as a buffoon, a comic character. This was the case even in the eighteenth century for Nicholas Rowe points out that "the part of the Jew (was) performed by an Excellent Comedian." Later in the same century he was played as a villain. Then the famous actor Edmund Kean presented him with great sympathy and sensitivity in the nineteenth century. Towards the end of the same century Henry Irving presented him as a noble and dignified character. He described Shylock as:

> The type of a persecuted race; almost the only gentleman in the play and the most ill-used.[13]

So by this time Shylock had become a dignified tragic figure.

If and when actors can bring about such a change in the portrayal of a character, literary critics can give even more interpretations. As a matter of fact, Shylock is not only one of the most discussed characters of this play, but in the entire work of Shakespeare. Anyone trying to understand this character should read at least the essays by E.E. Stoll and H.B. Charlton which present opposite views. One of the more modern interpretations sees Shylock linked with Antonio. According to Graham Midgeley both of them are studies in loneliness. Shylock is as lonely as Antonio is. In fact, more—for his daughter leaves him and after he is forcibly converted to Christianity, there can be no doubt that his own community will turn its back on him. Compared to this, Antonio's loneliness is as nothing. He will still have his Venetian friends and the support of Venetian society as well as the friendship of Bassanio and Portia, but Shylock will be totally abandoned.

Antonio

Antonio's position in the play is a very ambivalent one. The dramatist has named the play after him, yet one hesitates to call him the hero. There are several very valid reasons for this. First of all, there is the casket story which has great emotional appeal and secondly, in the bond story it is Shylock who dominates the plot, overshadowing Antonio. Therefore, though he is the merchant of Venice after whom the play has been named, he always takes the second place, and this makes one hesitate to call him the hero. Actually speaking, the one and only male character who remains in our memory is neither Antonio nor Bassanio but Shylock.

Antonio is the one character in the play who can be, only at the first and at a superficial level, be categorised as a "humour" character. The theory of Humours was a well-known theory of the time and the Melancholy Man was one of the basic humour characters. This theory is not very important as far as Shakespeare is concerned, for his characters are far too complex to be categorised as humour characters. Antonio, for example gives the impression of being a Melancholy Man in the beginning of the play and thereafter the typical features of such a character merge into that of a realistic portrayal. Some of the well-known features of the Melancholy Man are that he is a frustrated, disappointed man, railing at the world, at humanity and even at himself. One of the best portrayals of such a character has been given to us by Webster, in *The Duchess of Malfi,* in the character named Bosola. The only reasons that Antonio has been called a Melancholy Man is because, in the beginning of the play he has been portrayed as a man who is a prey to Melancholy without any discernible cause:

In sooth, I know not why I am so sad.
It wearies me, you say it wearies you;
But how I caught it, found it, or came by it
What stuff it's made of, whereof it is born
I am to learn.[14]

The two young men, Salarino and Solanio try to analyse and find out the cause, but it seems Antonio is not sad because he is worried about his merchandise, or because he is in love. So they solve the problem by saying that he is sad because he is not merry. After this we do not hear much about his melancholy. Instead, with Bassanio's entrance, the plot starts to take shape.

When we see him next we have already come to know that he is a devoted friend and also a man who lends money without taking any interest. He is quite outspoken with Shylock, telling him that the fact that he is borrowing money from him will not hold him back from insulting him. This outspokenness may be frank and honourable, but it is not wise. Shylock very cleverly appeals to his good nature by pretending to be friendly, and he is very easily taken in:

I will seal to such a bond
And say there is much kindness i'the Jew.[15]

Bassanio is more worldly-wise in distrusting Shylock. Antonio, however noble his nature might be, is much too gullible. Such men are invariably cheated by those who are less scrupulous than themselves.

Except for a brief appearance in the elopement scene, we see him next when he is put into prison by Shylock. The nobility of his nature manifests itself in this scene very clearly when he accepts his imprisonment and his inevitable doom with great calm. He wants Bassanio to come, not to rescue him, but to see how he pays his debt honourably.

Then comes the Trial scene. Antonio is merely a figure-head from here onwards. He conducts himself with great dignity throughout it but actually it is Portia's scene. It is only towards the end that he comes into prominence, when he forgives Shylock and poses the two conditions about making Lorenzo his heir and changing his religion. After this he recedes into the background, speaking only a few sentences in the last scene.

His character is not one that dwells in the memory. Heine dismisses him as "a weak creature without energy." This negative view, however, is not shared by everyone, for he has been regarded as the very symbol of the Roman concept of honour and also as a perfect character. Indeed, Bassanio describes him as such:

> [...] and one in whom
> The ancient Roman honour more appears
> Than any that draws breath in Italy.[16]

Not only this, he has been interpreted very seriously as the knight defending "the cause of disinterested generosity." Mark Van Doren looks upon him as a man who fights militantly against the custom of usury. He is the upholder of the Christian concept of morality, of charity, to the extent that he is ready to sacrifice himself. It has also been suggested that his deep love for Bassanio is the cause of his melancholy, for he feels that Bassanio has betrayed their friendship by falling in love with Portia and wanting to marry her.

An important aspect of this character has been highlighted by Graham Midgeley who thinks that both Antonio and Shylock are two sides of the same coin, for both are studies in loneliness:

> Visually one cannot escape the parallel between the lonely Shylock creeping from the stage [...] and this lonely Antonio walking from the stage, following without joy the triumphant pairs of lovers.[17]

In spite of these various views, however, many critics regard Antonio as the true hero of the play. W.H. Auden, along with many others, holds this view.

Bassanio

As far as his personality goes, Bassanio is the least important of the major characters, though, from the point of view of the plot, he is very important. First of all, he is the romantic hero of the play, whom the heroine falls in love with and marries. He is present in the two most important scenes of the play—the Casket scene and the Trial scene, in the former of which he is the central figure. Moreover, the two other male figures,

Antonio and Shylock, are not present in this scene at all. As a matter of fact he is present in no less than six scenes in the play, two of which are the crucial scenes, and no other male character can claim as much. In spite of all this, however, one still hesitates to put him even among the major characters, much less call him the hero of the play. This is because of his personality which does not command our respect and sympathy as Antonio's does, or fascinated horror and pity as Shylock's does.

He is a member of the Venetian high society, but it is quite clear that he is an irresponsible spendthrift and a fortune hunter. He has wasted his own money and has borrowed more money from Antonio. Now, after having spent what he had borrowed, he wants to borrow even more money in order to go to Belmont and court Portia. It is significant that in describing her the first thing he mentions is her wealth, "In Belmont there's a lady richly left." Her beauty and virtue are mentioned as the second and third of her attributes. He gives the impression of being one of those charming and entirely useless irresponsible young men of the aristocracy to be seen in so many plays and novels. They have nothing to do, cannot do anything, and do not want to do anything either.

Antonio offers him not only his money but his person as well as his reputation ("Try what my credit can in Venice do") and he takes it all. It is true that he tries to dissuade Antonio from signing the fatal bond, but, all the same, he does accept the money which has been procured by placing the very life of his friend in jeopardy.

After this, however, Shakespeare gives him better attributes. In the Casket scene he shines as the romantic hero, beloved of Portia. He rejects the gold casket and opts for the lead one, thereby winning Portia and also fulfilling the audience's expectations. It has been pointed out that he is not aware of the irony inherent in his rejection of the golden casket, when it was the gold he borrowed that has made all this at all possible for him. This objection is quite valid, but, then, it would not have been the right kind of thought for him. That is not the kind of nature he has. He is a happy-go-lucky young man. Had he suddenly developed intellectual and detached self-analysis, that would not have tallied with his nature. In other works, the Aristotelian requirement of consistency would not have been fulfilled.

After this his character gains even more in depth, for he rushes to Antonio's help, leaving his newly-won bride behind him. The duties of friendship, very properly, come first here. It is not a question of double loyalty for him. Though the Trial scene is more of Portia's scene than anyone else's, here also Bassanio shows up as a true friend, doing his level best to save Antonio. He parallels Antonio's earlier declaration of putting his money and his person in his hands, with one of his own:

> The Jew shall have my flesh, blood, bones and all
> Ere thou shalt lose for me one drop of blood.[18]

It has been suggested by cynical critics that these are but empty words, but there is no need to take them as such. Some critics take them as seriously meant.

Later, when Portia pretends to have taken umbrage at having been refused the ring and goes away, he sends the ring to her as soon as Antonio asks him to do so, thus proving his friendship and loyalty.

The character of Bassanio, thus, improves as the play proceeds, but he never has the status that either Antonio or Shylock, as dramatic characters, have. He is realistic enough and consistent within the limitations of his character. We see three aspects of his character: as an aristocrat gallant, as the romantic hero, and as a friend. These are not mutually exclusive. The unfolding of the personality, revealing these different aspects is completely believable.

These four major characters, thus, act out the main story of the play, they are each indispensable. Each is connected with the three important plots—the Bond plot, the Casket plot and the Ring episode. Yet it has to be kept in mind that the main characters, by themselves, are never enough. A fitting social background has to be suggested and this can be done only by the minor characters, and those hosts of characters designated as "attendants" or "retinue." They create the world against which the major characters act out their stories.

REFERENCES

1. Wilders, J., *op. cit.*, 73-74.
2. *The Merchant of Venice*, Act I, sc. ii, ll. 22-25.
3. Act IV, sc. i, ll. 321-22.
4. Act IV, sc. i, ll. 338-39.
5. Wilders, J., *op. cit.*, 167.
6. *Ibid.*, 162.
7. Act I, sc. iii, ll. 41-46.
8. Act II, sc. viii, ll. 15-16.
9. Act III, sc. i, ll. 67-75.
10. Wilders, J., *op. cit.*, 134.
11. Act IV, sc. i, ll. 395-97.
12. Wilders, *op. cit.*, 29.
13. *Ibid.*, 14.
14. Act I, sc. i, ll. 1-5.
15. Act II, sc. iii, ll. 151-52.
16. Act III, sc. ii, ll. 293-95.
17. Wilders, *op. cit.*, 207.
18. Act IV, sc. i, ll. 112-13.

7

THE MINOR CHARACTERS

One of the reasons for Shakespeare's supremacy over the other dramatists of his time is that even his minor characters are rounded out and realistic creations. Hardly any other dramatist can claim to have done as much. Marlowe, for example, created onc great character in one play—the Marlovian hero—and the other characters were sketches in a hasty, careless manner. His minor characters are shadowy creatures. This is not the case with Shakespeare. In his mature plays, as *The Merchant,* even the minor characters give an impression of realistic solidity and create a social background for the play. There are several minor characters in our play. Among the males are Gratiano, Lorenzo and the two young men Salarino and Solanio. Among the female characters there are Jessica and Nerissa. There are two servants, Launcelot Gobbo and his father (though the latter cannot really be called a servant). There is another character who makes a very brief appearance—Tubal who is designated as Shylock's friend.

Gratiano

Gratiano can be said to be the most important of the minor characters. He, along with Salarino and Solanio, is described as "friends to Antonio and Bassanio." He is the one who accompanies Bassanio to Belmont, marries Nerissa, the heroine's companion, accompanies Bassanio to the court and comes back to Belmont in the last scene. Thus he is present on the stage in all the important scenes as well as many others.

He is presented as a laughing, garrulous young man, a fit too light-hearted by temperament. He is shown as treasuring this trait of his personality:

Let me play the fool
With mirth and laughter let and wrinkles come.[1]

When necessary, however, he can be quite serious as he is when pleading with Bassanio to be allowed to accompany him to Belmont. Bassanio is doubtful whether he will be able to conduct himself properly at Belmont for he is "too wild, too rude and bold of voice." Gratiano, however, protests that his manners will be irreproachable, as indeed they are. In the Casket scene he keeps quiet till the choosing is over and Portia and Bassanio have declared their love for each other. It is a solemn occasion and his manners are suitably grave and sober.

Though he is light-hearted, this lightness does not extend to his love. He has been constant and serious in his love:

You saw the mistress, I beheld the maid;
You lov'd, I lov'd; for intermission
No more pertains to me, my lord, than you.[2]

He has the social graces usual in his class. When Lorenzo and Jessica come to Belmont he realizes that Jessica will be feeling shy and awkward, so he directs Nerissa to look after her.

After this we see him in the Trial scene, faithfully accompanying Bassanio. He too pleads with Shylock to have mercy. There is no jesting and fooling here, for the occasion is far too serious for any humorous comments. When, however, the scene reaches its turning-point, he cannot control himself and breaks out with ironic comments. He has been severely criticised for gloating and jeering at a fallen enemy and baiting him, but it must be remembered that the Elizabethan groundlings may not have had as keen a sense of honour as the sophisticated modern reader has. Their viewpoint was different and Gratiano's attitude might have reflected their own.

Gratiano has not been seriously taken by most of Shakespeare's readers, but there are some who have interpreted him as representing the shallow worldly-wiseness of affluent and sophisticated Venetian society. He is full of witticism and shallow cynicism. For example he does not take Antonio's sadness at all seriously. It is as if Antonio is merely pretending to be sad in order to deceive others. He simply does not have the depth to be able to sympathise with Antonio. In fact he mocks at him:

> There are a sort of men, whose visages
> Do cream and mantle like a standing bond,
> And do a wilful stillness entertain,
> With purpose to be dress'd in an opinion
> Of wisdom, gravity profound conceit;
> As who should say, "I am Sir Oracle,
> And when I open my lips let no dog bark."[3]

He is witty, fond of playing with words and seems to be bent on exhibiting all that is vain and shallow in human nature, including the baseness that jeers at a defeated enemy:

> In all this Gratiano makes explicit the attitude of the worldly Christian, revealing in a crude and unmistakenable form what is more subtly present in the rest.[4]

This is a very severe interpretation of his character. One cannot say what Shakespeare's own view was. This play does not have the character of a clown, or a fool. It is certain that Gratiano provides the touch of light-hearted wittiness often supplied by the clown. Certainly he fills the post of Bassanio's companion adequately just as Nerissa does with Portia. Gratiano thus fulfils two dramatic purposes: he provides highgrade clowning and is also Bassanio's companion.

Lorenzo

The next important minor character is Lorenzo. It is true that he has not been pointed out as the friend of Antonio and Bassanio. Perhaps this is because he has another identity, that of being Jessica's lover. It is clear, however, that he belongs to the same social circle of affluent light-hearted young men to which Antonio and Bassanio belong. Not only does he fill up the social background, but he has also got a special significance, for he is the hero of the subplot. This is the capacity in which he has been described in the list of the *Dramatis Personae*—as Jessica's lover, not as Bassanio's friend. It is a significant fact that he is entirely Shakespeare's own creation. There is no such character in the sources he used.

As such, he is an honourable and serious young man, for he does not take his love-affair at all callously. He plans to elope with Jessica but he is seriously in love with her and appreciates her worth. This becomes apparent in the elopement scene:

> Beshrew me, but I love her heartily;
> For she is wise, if I can judge of her,
> And fair she is, if that mine eyes be true,
> And therefore like herself, fair, wise and true,
> Shall she be placed in my constant soul.[5]

It is a remarkable fact that neither here, nor elsewhere, does Lorenzo show himself to be concerned with the money that Jessica steals from Shylock and brings with her. Bassanio, when speaking of Portia, mentions her wealth first. From Shylock we hear everlastingly of money. Lorenzo, however, never speaks of it. In the scene between Shylock and Tubal we come to know how the run-away couple have frittered away their money, but it is always Jessica who has been spending her stolen money, never Lorenzo. He has not, like Bassanio, turned to a bride with money. Instead, he has turned to a girl who is sure to be cast out by her father and, moreover, carries the stigma of being a Jewess. It is true that she will be converted to Christianity, but the stigma will nevertheless be there. Yet he never mentions these facts. In a way, he is far more the ideal lover than Bassanio is.

His love for Jessica, however serious it might be, has not deprived him of humour. The famous moonlit scene is an example of it, for, in addition to sincere love, it also has the element of humour in it. He and Jessica cap each other's description of the moonlit night with examples from classical mythology till Lorenzo refers to their own elopement. Jessica replies wittily and humorously and Lorenzo, readily responding to the change in tone, replies:

> In such a night
> Did pretty Jessica, like a little shrew
> Slander her love, and he forgave it her.[6]

This is a down-to-earth realistic love, not the idealized courtly love that has no contact with everyday life. This is to be seen very often in Elizabethan plays—there are different degrees of love. The chief characters, that is Bassanio-Portia, Rosalind-Orlando, Viola-Orsino, express a heightened, courtly love, whereas the minor pairs have a slightly more earthy and lighter kind of love. In this play, in like manner, we have the same gradation. Shakespeare uses humour to tone down the intensity of love. It is none the less sincere for that.

Shakespeare, moreover, has given the soul of a poet to Lorenzo. It is rarely that a character speaks as beautifully of nature and music as Lorenzo does. First we have the wonderful sky-scape:

> Look how the floor of heaven
> Is thick inlaid with patines of bright gold.
> There's not the smallest orb which thou behold'st,
> But in his motion like an angel sings,
> Still quiring to the young-eyed cherubins;
> Such harmony is in immortal souls;
> But whilst this muddy vesture of decay,
> Doth grossly close't in, we cannot hear it.[7]

Here in this speech Lorenzo describes both the starry sky and the supernatural music of the spheres. Another later speech describes the effect of music upon the hearers and concludes:

> The man that hath no music in himself
> Nor is not mov'd with concord of sweet sounds,
> Is fit for treason, stratagems and spoils;
> The motions of his spirit are dull as night
> And his affections dark as Erebus,
> Let no such man be trusted.[8]

Shakespeare would not have given Lorenzo such lines if he had not meant him to be of a frank and open nature.

The only clue we have to his financial status comes right at the end. He comes to know how he has been made Shylock's heir, and bursts out:

> Fair ladies, you drop manna in the way of starv'd people.[9]

This makes it clear that he is an impecunious youth with a not too bright and secure future, so the assurance of inheriting a sizable fortune is very welcome. Yet we are never made conscious of this fact as happens repeatedly with Bassanio.

Not everyone, however, views Lorenzo favourably. The objection has been made that their attitude to love has no change or development:

> Jessica and Lorenzo are stylized in that they never waver in their devotion [...] they leave little room for growth in their conception of love and their awareness of its power.[10]

It has also been pointed out by Sigurd Burckhardt that the love of Lorenzo and Jessica is the opposite of the love of Bassanio and Portia, for it is based on theft and elopement. Shakespeare, however, treats them leniently. Perhaps this is because Lorenzo is entirely his brain-child.

Salarino and Solanio

These two characters are hardly to be distinguished from each other. They are almost always together and it is only very rarely that they are separated from each other. Solanio appears in the elopement scene by himself and so does Solanio at the end of the casket scene. In the next scene, where Antonio is being put into prison, Salarino is with him. Except for these three scenes they are always together.

Together they represent a whole world—the world of the wealthy and magnificent Venetians of whom Antonio and Bassanio are members. Harley Granville-Barker is of the opinion that this is the important function they fulfil:

> They are there to paint Venice for us, the
> Venice of the magnificent young men.[11]

These two affluent, high-spirited young men are cultured and talk in a highly polished manner, with classical allusions that fall naturally from their lips. Antonio by himself, or with Bassanio as well, would not have been able to create the world of sophisticated Venice as successfully as these two do.

They have some other important functions to fulfil. Granville-Barker has given a list of these: first of all, it is through them that the audience first hears of the disasters that have struck Antonio's ventures in the first scene of the third Act:

> Why, yet it lives there uncheck'd, that Antonio hath a ship of rich lading wrack'd on th'narrow seas.[12]

Later in the same scene they provoke Shylock into his famous outburst. They show a callous indifference to his mental turmoil. This, however, reflects the contemporary attitude of the Christians. They, too, represent the ordinary man's common sense view of the bond:

> Why, I am sure, if he forfeit, thou wilt not take his flesh: what is that good for?[13]

Then later in the next scene, which is the casket scene, Solanio brings the letter from Antonio and gives Bassanio the news of Antonio's misfortunes, and also how Shylock is standing adamant over his bond. These details tell Bassanio, Portia and the audience of the danger threatening Antonio:

> The duke himself, the magnificoes
> Of greatest port, have all persuaded him
> But none can drive him from the envious plea
> Of forfeiture, of justice, and his bond.[14]

Both of them are present in the Trial scene, but they hardly speak, except to announce Shylock and then the disguised Portia. With that, their usefulness ends and they are not present in the last Act. They belong to Venice and therefore they remain there and do not come to Belmont. Their intrusion in the moonlit night Belmont would have struck a discordant note. These two characters, who barely differ from each other, are used with great economy and though they do not contribute to the action yet, in their own way, are both quite indispensable.

Tubal

Introduced as Shylock's friend Tubal appears just once. He had, presumably, been sent to Genoa to find about all that he could about the runaway couple Lorenzo and Jessica. In this scene he enters a little after Shylock's terrible speech and brings him news about his daughter as well as Antonio. The scene has been looked upon as a comic one, for he tells Shylock alternately about Jessica and Antonio, and Shylock reacts accordingly: with lamentation when he hears about Jessica and joy when he hears about Antonio. The alternation of these does produce a comic effect, but this does not mean that Tubal intends to torture Shylock. He is a Jew, and Shylock's friend. It is to be supposed that he wants to spare Shylock any pain. It is noticeable that he speaks about Jessica only when Shylock asks, but as soon as Shylock responds with anger and grief, he quickly tries to divert him with news about Antonio. He has to tell Shylock all the news he has gathered about Jessica, but he tries to alleviate it by voluntarily offering him information about Antonio. He tries to keep up Shylock's spirits.

He serves two useful functions: he provides the only inkling of a Jewish background, a Jewish community behind Shylock, and also gives us news about Antonio, Lorenzo and Jessica. Not much individuality is given to him, but there is no reason to think of him as a puppet-master, pulling Shylock this way and that by giving him different pieces of news. He can, instead be regarded as really a friend who tries to keep up Shylock's spirits by giving him good news (that is, what Shylock's will regard as good news) along with bad news.

Jessica

Jessica is definitely the more important of the two minor female characters. She is the heroine of the subplot and her social standing, in her own community, is above that of Nerissa who is just a waiting-woman. Whatever Shakespeare's own attitude to her might have been, neither her speech nor her actions endear her to modern critics. She proves to be disloyal to her father, steals his money and jewellery and elopes in an immodest manner, disguised as a boy. She is the first female character in the play to don a disguise and she does so in order to make her elopement easier, that is, to serve a personal end. When we see her first she is already arranging for her elopement and shows a momentary shamefaced consciousness of her disloyalty to her father:

> Alack, what heinous sin it is in me
> To be asham'd to be my father's child.[15]

But after this there is never any repetition of this twinge of conscience. There is not a loyal bone in her body.

There is no doubt a positive side to her behaviour. It can be said that she is ready to sacrifice every thing for love. She leaves the security of her parental home, her social position in her own community and her religion in order to escape ignominiously with Lorenzo to face a doubtful future. She shows herself to be a heartless minx in betraying her father and a soulless renegade forsaking her religion, but at least she is unwavering in her love.

There are some misgivings in her mind at the moment of elopement for she is not as sure of her lover as she would like to be, but after this, it is to be presumed, there are no heart-burnings. She carelessly fritters away the money she had stolen from her father, spending four score ducats in one night in Genoa and buying a monkey with the turquoise ring sacred to the memory of her mother. It is not surprising that F.E. Halliday should call her "a turncoat and a thief."[16] That is exactly what she is.

The only redeeming features that Shakespeare has given her are a sense of humour and total freedom from any kind of jealously. This latter trait is seen when the two of them arrive at Belmont and are left in charge of Portia's house. She likes Portia "Past all expressing" and declare:

> the poor rude world
> Hath not her fellow in't.[17]

This is said in spite of the fact that Lorenzo openly admires Portia. It goes to show that there is no cattiness in her.

The moonlit scene shows her at her best—light-hearted, witty and humorous, she gives the impression of being secure and happy in her love. The scene begins on a note of high, idealised lyrical love, with Jessica making her own contribution. Then humour and realism creeps in through her rejoinder to Lorenzo:

> In such a night
> Did young Lorenzo swear he lov'd her well
> Stealing her soul with many vows of faith
> And ne'er a true one.[18]

After this, except for one brief speech, she recedes into the background. Even the news of Lorenzo's having been made Shylock's heir does not call forth any response from her. This is not surprising, for she had betrayed him most shamefully. Any protestations of care at his misfortunes will sound like rank hypocrisy from a daughter as undutiful as she has proved to be.

Nerissa

The waiting-woman of Portia, Nerissa is the next female character. Even though she is very much of a yes-woman, yet Shakespeare has given her individuality without whom Portia cannot move a step. It was absolutely necessary for a girl, specially if she was unmarried, to have another older woman with her, not only to keep her company, but also to guard her. This custom of having a chaperone or a duenna had continued down to the nineteenth century. Nerissa fills this post, but with a difference. She cannot be much older than Portia, since Gratiano, who is Bassanio's friend, marries her. Thus, she is more of a friend or companion than either a chaperone or a servant. Portia is alone in her great house. There are many servants to do her biddings, but they are all servants. They cannot give her company, relieve the monotony of her life, advise her and console her in her hour of need. All this is the work of a lady-companion. Such a companion did not have much liberty of action and neither has Nerissa. She has to do her mistress's bidding. Yet, ever then, her life is not a miserable one, for she and Portia seem to be of the same age and there is a very friendly relationship between them.

The fact that Shakespeare has given her individuality becomes apparent with the very first sentence she speaks. Portia says that she has got tired of the world. The modern reader at once understands this as the boredom from which persons who have nothing to do suffer. Nerissa does not give a sycophantic response. Instead she says:

> You would be, sweet madam, if your miseries were in the same abundance as your good fortunes are. And yet, for aught I see, they are as sick that surfeit with too much as they that starve with nothing.[19]

This is mild rebuke to Portia and, for a dependent companion, bold on Nerissa's part. It is her good fortune that Portia recognizes the good sense in her words. It also speaks volumes for Portia's own good nature.

After this Nerissa serves the extremely useful purpose of acquainting the reader with the terms of Portia's father's will. This is a bit of necessary information which has to be imparted to the reader and Shakespeare has chosen her to be the vehicle. It is difficult to see how else it could have been done, for, if it had been left to Portia the only chance she would have had would have been to tell her suitors at the moment of choosing. This she will do, later, in any case. Yet, at such a time, her own attitude would not have become clear. When the two girls discuss the whole business then she can voice her own mild objections.

Nerissa next performs the important task of informing the reader about the suitors who have come to court Portia. She frankly asks Portia about her attitude towards them. The suitors who have already come are then described by her and Portia's witty responses signify her annoyance. It is after this that Nerissa mentions Bassanio and once more we become aware of her usefulness, for there is nobody else who could have done this work of recalling Bassanio to Portia's mind, and that also with favourable overtones:

> [...] he, of all the men that my foolish eyes looked upon, was the best deserving of a fair lady.[20]

In this scene, where she appears for the first time, thus, she is seen as an individual and also as a highly useful figure, undertaking those functions that could have been fulfilled only by her—the confidante and chaperone of the heroine.

It is not clear whether she is present on the stage with Portia in the scene in which the Prince of Morocco makes his choice. She is not mentioned by name in the stage-directions, nor does she speak, but it is to be assumed that she is always present by the side of Portia, whether mentioned or not. Later she is definitely present in the Casket scene (that is, the scene in which Bassanio makes his choice). It is to be noted that it is she who first congratulates Portia, not Gratiano. Then, after Gratiano has announced their own intentions to marry and Portia asks her if it is true or not, she answers in a short and modest line. Thereafter she remains silent, as is but fitting for one in her position. She speaks only when she is alone with Portia, not if there are other characters present.

Next comes the scene in which Portia makes her plans. She entrusts her household to Lorenzo and Jessica and then unfolds her plant to Nerissa. Nerissa acquiesces to these plans, without voicing any misgivings or cautions. Portia is so overflowing with enthusiasm that it is she who speaks, and Nerissa merely agrees.

In the Trial scene she is the lawyer's clerk and as such does exactly what she is required to do. This scene is Portia's scene and she echoes Portia when Gratiano, like Bassanio, makes protestations of friendship and sacrifice towards Antonio. One can be sure that here also she speaks because Portia speaks to Bassanio in a like manner.

When, after the trial is over, Portia is trying unsuccessfully to get her ring back from Bassanio, she keeps quiet, but when Gratiano brings the ring to Portia, she too tries to get her own ring from him. Shakespeare knew the limitations of a waiting-woman's activities and makes Nerissa observe them quite scrupulously. Incidentally, we have not been told when and how Nerissa gave Gratiano her ring. Perhaps it was in the Casket scene itself, in a mute side-show. Here (Act IV, sc. ii) she mentions it quite clearly.

It is in the last scene that she again comes into prominence with the Ring episode. It is in line no. 141 that the quarrel between her and Gratiano starts. They draw the main characters' attention to themselves by starting to talk in loud voices. Nerissa pretends not to believe Gratiano when he says he had given the ring to a lawyer's clerk, and accuses him of having given it to a girl. Her words are fraught with dramatic irony:

> Gave it to a judge's clerk! no, God's my judge
> The clerk will never wear hair on his face that had it.[21]

These words have a double meaning perfectly understood and enjoyed by the reader. Nerissa shows herself worthy of her husband who is himself so very fond of playing with words.

After this, however, the focus shifts to the main characters and Nerrisa speaks only to echo and support Portia in every thing she says. Then, after Portia has revealed the secret of their disguise she hands Lorenzo the deed of gift whereby he becomes Shylock's heir.

Nerissa thus, though rather like a shadow of Portia, echoing her every move, has yet been given individuality within her limited scope and is a highly useful character from the dramatic point of view.

Launcelot Gobbo

Launcelot belongs to a class of characters different from the ones studied so far—he is a servant. Servants, however, fill important positions in comedies. In classical Roman comedies servants are the intriguers in the play. They are clever rogues, managing the affairs of their masters, helping them in their escapades and generally making themselves indispensable to the plot. Ben Jonson follows this tradition from the very beginning of his career, for example in creating Brainworm in *Every Man in His Humour* and many others such later on. Launcelot Gobbo, however, is not a servant of that type. He is a smart rogue, but nowhere near Jonson's Face or Mosca. The only intrigue in which he helps is to carry Jessica's letter to Lorenzo—he himself is no intriguer.

He is shown as partly clown and partly an opportunistic servant. He leaves Shylock's service for no other reason that serving under Bassanio will offer a better life. He is lazy and unscrupulous and Shylock's strictures on him seem to be fully justified.

The most important aspect of Launcelot is that of the clown, making the audience laugh. He is the low comedian as supplementing the role of the high comedian Gratiano. Like his noble counterpart, Launcelot, too, is fond of playing with words, though in his case it is the misuse of words that provokes laughter. A few instances are:

(a) my heels are at your commandment
(b) the Jew is the very devil incarnation
(c) as my father [...] shall fructify unto you
(d) in very brief, the suit is impertinent to myself.[22]

All these, and many more, occur in one scene alone. Everything about him, and not merely his words, is designed to provoke laughter. The initial dialogue between his conscience and the fiend, then the dialogue between his father and himself—all belong to the tradition of clowning. It is not clowning at a very high level, nor is he one of those famous

Fools of Shakespeare who are wiser than their masters. He, however, serves the purpose of a low-grade comedian quite effectively. The character of the buffoon or the clown is one of the classical requirements in a comedy and Launcelot fulfils this requirement.

The minor characters of *The Merchant*, thus, are, for the most part, given due importance. They are sketched in briefly but effectively. Each has his or her own contribution to make to the action and the mood of the play. However minor they might be, they cannot be dispensed with. More than anything else, they show with what artistry and economy Shakespeare uses even the humblest character to serve his dramatic purposes.

REFERENCES

1. *The Merchant of Venice*, Act I, sc. i, ll. 79-80.
2. Act III, sc. ii, ll. 198-200.
3. Act I, sc. i, ll. 88-94.
4. Moody, A.D., *Shakespeare: The Merchant of Venice*. Studies in English Literature series, no. 21. London: Edward Arnold (Publishers) Ltd., 1964, 22.
5. Act II, sc. vi, ll. 52-56.
6. Act V, sc. i, ll. 20-22.
7. Act V, sc. i, ll. 58-65.
8. Act V, sc. i, ll. 83-88.
9. Act V, sc. i, ll. 294-95.
10. Champion, L.S., *The Evolution of Shakespeare's Comedies: A Study in Dramatic Perspective*. Harvard: The Univ. Press, 1970, 63.
11. Wilders, J., *op. cit.*, 70.
12. Act III, sc. i, ll. 2-4.
13. Act III, sc. i, ll. 50-51.
14. Act III, sc. ii, ll. 278-92.
15. Act II, sc. iii, ll. 16-17.
16. Halliday, F.E., *op. cit.*, 130.
17. Act III, sc. v, ll. 79-80.
18. Act V, sc. i, ll. 17-20.
19. Act I, sc. ii, ll. 3-7.
20. Act I, sc. ii, ll. 117-18.
21. Act V, sc. i, ll. 157-58.
22. (a) Act II, sc. ii, ll. 30-31, (b) Act II, sc. ii, l. 26, (c) Act II, sc. ii, ll. 127-28, (d) Act II, sc. ii, ll. 131-32.

8
DRAMATIC STRUCTURE/PLOT

Comedies, usually, have complex structure-patterns, for, as a rule, they have many intrigues. Elizabethan comedies, usually, have more than one plot and several intrigues and episodes. In this connection, certain basic ideas should be kept in mind, for these were not only well-known in Shakespeare's time, but the dramatists were more or less expected to observe them. As is to be seen in Aristotle's definition (given in Chapter 6, *supra*), he does not have anything to say about plot in comedy, for the main stress there is on character. Elsewhere in the *Poetics,* however, he has said much about plot and these apply to comedy as well as to tragedy.

The Classical Rules and *The Merchant of Venice*

The rule of the unities: These rules had supposedly been handed down from Aristotle by his classical commentators. There are three of these rules: (a) the Unity of Action, (b) Unity of Time and (c) Unity of Place. It is necessary to understand these first, though it should be remembered that, most of the time, Shakespeare did not observe them.

(a) *The Unity of Action:* Properly speaking, Unity of Action means that there should be no mingling of serious and comic actions in the one and the same play. The rule is usually held to be relevant for tragedies, but it is pertinent to comedies as well. Just as there should be no comic action in a tragedy, so there should not be any serious action in a comedy. Such a play should contain only light-hearted action—satirical ones in the case of satirical comedy and romantic ones in the case of romantic comedy. This second kind of play can contain satirical elements, or action provoking derisive laughter, for such scenes are not counted as tragic scenes, though the moral intent is serious. Any scene or action, however, which provokes sorrow or pity has no place in a comedy, for such emotions belong to tragedy.

In *The Merchant* the fate of Shylock proves to be a problem, for he faces a tragic sequel to all his plans. The impression of tragedy is so strong in his case that it has been remarked upon down the ages. Nicholas Rowe called the play a tragedy and there are many defences of Shylock by many critics. His fate invites our pity and this goes totally against the law of unity of action. It needs the full strength of Shakespeare's poetry in the last scene to bring about a happy ending after the Trial scene, so strong is the effect of Shylock's tragedy.

(b) *The Unity of Time:* This rule requires that the actual story of the play should not cover more than one day. Aristotle himself uses the phrase "a single revolution of the sun" to mark out the time limit. This is a very difficult goal to achieve, but not impossible. Ben Jonson was a thorough neo-classicist and observed all the rules. His plays usually take place within one day, starting in the morning and ending in the evening. He was, however, the only contemporary of Shakespeare who had observed all these rules. Shakespeare himself hardly ever did so. The most flagrant violation of the unity of time is to be found in *The Winter's Tale* where more than sixteen years are covered in the play.

It is not very sure exactly how much time has been covered in our play, but it is definitely a little more than three months. This is the length of time allowed in the bond:

Shylock : Three thousand ducats,—well.
Bassanio : Ay, Sir, for three months.
Shylock : For three months,—well.[1]

This is repeated a few more times. After the expiry of these three months during which Antonio has been unable to pay back the money he is put into prison and the trial takes place. What is not certain is how many days after the three months does the trial take place. Immediately after the trial Portia comes back to Belmont and the play ends. It is safe, therefore, to assume that three months and a few more days are covered by the action of the play.

(c) *The Unity of Place:* This rule means that the action of play should take place in one and the same place. Again, this would seem to be quite impossible, because, even a strict neoclassicist like Ben Jonson has allowed a few changes of scenes in his plays. In *The Alchemist,* for example, the action takes place in the same house, but in different rooms, the adjoining garden and the street just outside the front-door of the house. The other Elizabethan playwrights did not care so much and Shakespeare certainly did not.

In *The Merchant* the action takes place mainly in two locations—Venice and Belmont. Within these locations, again, there are many changes of scenes. In Venice itself, for example, there is the street in the first scene, then Shylock's house and also the court-room in the Trial scene. At Belmont, different rooms in Portia's house have been used. It is to be presumed, though, that all the three Casket scenes take place in the same room. In addition, in the last scene the garden has been used. There are, thus, several changes of scenes.

It should be borne in mind that neo-classical critics had criticized Shakespeare very severely for his violation of these three unities. Dr. Johnson, however had defended these flaws and they seem outmoded and insignificant in modern times. They, however, and the other classical rules were the only rules of drama known in the times of Shakespeare. The violation of, or, on the other hand, careful observance of the rules was important in those days. It is a proof of Shakespeare's genius that in his own time itself he was regarded as a master dramatist, in spite of having flouted all rules.

Besides these three unities, there are certain other important classical rules known and followed by the Elizabethans. There was a famous treatise on drama by the Italian critic Donatus which was prescribed in those days. Donatus, like all classical critics, was a follower of Aristotle. He not only accepted Aristotle's maxims but elaborated them as well. The Elizabethans, for the most part, did not have much knowledge of Aristotle at first hand. So they followed the later critics like Horace and others. Donatus gives very precise rules about plays. According to him there are five stages or parts in plot, which actually boils down to three: Prologue, Protasis, Epitasis, Catastrophe and Epilogue. The Five-Act scheme fits easily into this pattern:

Prologue	:	Some dramatists give it before the actual action begins, as in classical plays. When such is not the case then usually it is the first scene.
Protasis	:	Acts I and II.
Epitasis	:	Acts III and IV.
Catastrophe	:	Act V.
Epilogue	:	Sometimes given separately. Usually it is the last scene or speech in the play.

These divisions, however, were not water-tight compartments. Sometimes the Protasis may finish in the first Act itself and in that case the Epitasis will be quite long. In some plays the Epitasis may spread over into the fifth Act and the Catastrophe may come only in the last scene.

The Prologue, when given separately, usually tells about the theme and the story. Marlowe's Prologue to *Dr. Faustus* is of this kind. Shakespeare but rarely wrote Prologues. There are only three plays in which separate Prologues are given—*Henry VIII, Troilus and Cressida,* and *Romeo and Juliet.* These have Prologues before the actual start of the play, specifically so designated. Three others, *Henry IV Pt. II, Henry V* and *Pericles* have speeches by the Chorus or others, preceding the play, but not named as Prologues. In *The Merchant of Venice* the first part of the first scene may be considered to be in the nature of a Prologue though not a proper Prologue at all.

The Protasis introduces all the main characters and the action begins. In *The Merchant* the first Act is the Protasis, for, in its three scenes the main characters have been introduced and the beginnings of the Casket story as well as the Bond story are seen.

The Epitasis is the main body of the play. Here all the intrigues and episodes take place. Complications are introduced. Then there comes a point when the complications reach such a climatic point that the issue seems to be doubtful. This climatic point is known as the summa Epitasis. In *The Merchant* the central three Acts make up the Epitasis and the climatic point is reached in the Trial scene, when Antonio's fate hangs in the balance.

The Catastrophe is that part of the play in which all

complexities are smoothed out and, in comedies, the happy ending, as expected, takes place. In our play the last Act, comprising only one scene, is the Catastrophe. Today the word "catastrophe," as in ordinary use, has taken on a negative meaning. In this context, however, it merely means the end.

Donatus's description of these divisions is very illuminating. He says that the Protasis is "brisk" and the Epitasis is "stomy," the Catastrophe is "almost tragic." Yet all these troubles come, specially in romantic comedies, to a soothing and enjoyable conclusion. This description fits the Act-divisions of our play like a glove. It has been pointed out by numerous writers that Shylock's fate is tragic and that the entire play trembles on the verge of a tragedy. Yet Donatus himself has said that the Catastrophe is "almost tragic." Moreover, Donatus say this with reference to the main character. *The Merchant* being a romantic comedy, Shylock, however important and unique he might be, cannot take the place of the hero. As such, therefore, Shakespeare's Catastrophe is quite in the classically approved manner, for tragedy almost touches Antonio, but balance is restored and the play ends happily for all, except for Shylock.

From the classical point of view, therefore, we see that this play has violated the unities, for even the unity of action, the most important of the three, is endangered by the treatment meted out to Shylock. As far as the Donatun divisions are concerned, the play is quite regular.

These, however, were not all the classical rules for comedy. There were a few other principles well-known to Shakespeare and his contemporaries. One such principle is Peripeteia or the Reversal of fortunes. This feature usually has a negative meaning and gives complexity to drama, whether tragedy or comedy. In comedy however, reversal from good fortune to ill fortune does not last. Circumstances change and the reversal is itself reversed, that is, good fortune again smiles on the character and the play ends happily. Antonio falls from a high status in life to a low one. His ships are wrecked so he cannot meet the deadline for repaying Shylock, and his very life is in danger. But this state of affairs does not last and he gets everything back:

Sweet Lady, you have given me life and living
For here I read for certain that my ships
Are safely come to road.[2]

It is far otherwise for Shylock, but then he is the villain. In his case Peripeteia is an enduring feature. There is no recovery, all that he loses, he loses for ever.

There is, thus, double Peripeteia in *The Merchant,* a temporary one for Antonio and a permanent one for Shylock. Aristotle had said that a play without Peripeteia is simple drama and one with Peripeteia is complex. According to this rule, then, *The Merchant* is a complex play.

Another important dramatic element is Anagnorisis or Recognition. At its simplest, this will mean the mutual recognition of characters who have been separated. We have many recognitions of this kind in Shakespeare, a very good example being the Recognition-scene in *Twelfth Night,* where Viola and Sebastian recognise each other. This element is not present in any remarkable manner in our play. A very crude and simple recognition occurs between Launcelot Gobbo's father and himself, providing occasion for laughter. Portia and Nerissa's disguises are not penetrated. As a matter of fact it is on their *not* being recognised that the success of the play depends. When finally Portia reveals the secret the scene can be called a revelation, but not recognition.

The device of the *deus ex machina* is another classical strategy for bringing about a happy ending. This phrase means "god in a machine." Very often, in classical plays, a god, usually Apollo, would be brought on the stage to mete out justice and smooth out all difficulties. This important function is often given to ordinary human characters in Elizabethan plays. In our play the function of the *deus ex machina* is carried out by Portia in the Trial scene. At the last possible moment she saves Antonio's life and punishes Shylock. Usually the work of the *deus ex machina* is carried out by a person of authority like the King, or a judge, or someone like that. Shakespeare has shown innovation in entrusting this work to a young girl. It should be remembered, however, that Portia is not just a young girl in the Trial scene. She is a lawyer, with the full authority of the renowned and wise lawyer Dr. Bellario to support her.

Certain Elizabethan Features in *The Merchant*

An important feature of the New Classical Comedies and Elizabethan plays is that they have more than one plot. This is not the case with the old classical comedies. It is in the later comedies (Terence, for example) that two plots are to be found. The Elizabethans carried on this tradition. Ben Jonson's plays, for example, are not only double-plotted, but many of them are multiple-plotted. Shakespeare's plays, following the popular tendency, are double or multiple-plotted. Such plays require intelligence as well as ingenuity.

The Merchant of Venice is a play with three plots in it: the Bond plot of Antonio and Shylock, the Romantic plot of Bassanio and Portia, and the secondary Romantic plot of Lorenzo and Jessica. The intrigue about the rings at the end of the play cannot be called a subplot, it is an episode. Briefly, the Bond plot shows Antonio standing guarantee for Bassanio who borrows three thousand ducats from Shylock for three months. On failure to pay this sum within the stipulated time, a pound of flesh from Antonio's body is to be given as forfeit. This plot vies for the position of the main plot with the Casket plot. It is full of unexpected surprises, for news comes that all of Antonio's ships have foundered so he cannot pay Shylock back and the latter then claims the forfeit. This plot comes to a happy end through the resourcefulness of Portia though it ends tragically for Shylock, who, through a legal quibble, loses everything.

The Casket plot is the primary romantic plot. Here we see Bassanio choosing the right casket and winning Portia. After this, attention shifts to Antonio.

The third plot is the romantic plot of Lorenzo and Jessica. The two of them elope, marry and come to Belmont where everyone congregates at the end.

All these plots go to make *The Merchant of Venice* a multiple-plotted, complex structure. The relationship between these three plots will be studied more in detail after this. For the present it should be remembered that there is no provision in Aristotle for two or multiple-plotted plays. Though it existed in New Classical Comedies (for example Plautus and Terence) this is a feature developed to great complexity mainly by the

Elizabethans and our play is a typical Elizabethan comedy so far as this feature goes.

The use of disguise is another typical Elizabethan feature. This device is used to bring about the elements of complexity, surprise, dramatic irony and tension in the play. It is particularly for the sake of winning their beloved that the female characters in the romantic comedies disguise themselves. Shakespeare excelled in the use of disguises, specially the disguise of the heroine:

> [...] his most constant and successful use is that of the page's doublet and hose for the heroine.[3]

Such disguises were very conventional because in those days young boys acted female roles. So the longer the heroine is in disguise the more freedom the boy-actor had. There is much complexity here. The audience knows that it is a boy who is playing the role and so when the character dons a disguise things get even more complicated. M.C. Bradbrook is of the opinion that these disguises of the heroine into a boy:

> [...] enlarges the original role, and also discovers its latent possibilities.[4]

In this play all the three female characters disguise themselves into boys. Jessica is the first to do so. She disguises herself as a boy and joins Lorenzo's masquerade as his torch-bearer. Here the disguise is adopted to facilitate her elopement. Shakespeare makes good use of this opportunity to raise a laugh. Jessica feels shy which in itself is ironical, for she is indulging in an immoral action, of which she should be truly ashamed. The disguise is a much slighter thing:

> I am glad 'tis night, yet do not look on me
> For I am much asham'd of my exchange;
> But love is blind, and lovers cannot see
> The pretty follies that themselves commit.[5]

Such disguise gave much scope to the boy-actor for good acting.

Portia, however, is not acting out of self-interest. She disguises herself in order to save Antonio. Her disguise is not only purely unselfish and altruistic, it also serves a most important purpose in the play. It is this disguise that helps her in bringing about a happy ending to the Bond plot. Nerissa's disguise is in obedience to Portia; it, too is unselfish and altruistic. Herein Portia differs from the other Shakespearean heroines. Rosalind of *As You Like It* disguises herself in order to travel safely, and so does Celia in the same play. Viola in *Twelfth Night* dons the disguise of a page-boy because she wants safety and a job in the Duke's court at Illyria. Shakespeare, however, does not highlight Portia's altruistic motive. Instead he makes Portia take the whole business in a very light-hearted way:

I'll hold thee any wager
I'll prove the prettier fellow of the two;
And wear my dagger with the braver grace
And speak between the change of man and boy
With a reed voice.[6]

The change back into their own selves later, also, is not highlighted. When Portia reveals the mystery of their disguise it is done in very few words. It is definite, however, that *The Merchant* makes more effective and useful use of the convention of disguise than any other play of Shakespeare. Of the three disguises, Portia's is the most important as it affects the plot directly.

The Sources of *The Merchant of Venice*

Most of the plots of Shakespeare are taken from other plays existing before or from stories by other authorities. This is not to be adversely criticised as lack of originality, for such was the usual custom in those days. The mastery of the dramatist lay in what use he made of the material with which he constructed his own plays. Shakespeare takes a story or another play as his foundation and then alters it in several ways to suit his own dramatic requirements and purposes.

The plot of *The Merchant* has been taken mainly from three sources.[7] G. Bullough has given no less than eight sources. These are, in the order given by him:

(1) Ser Giovanni's *Il Pecorone.*

(2) Robert Wilson's *The Three Ladies of London.*

(3) A Silvyan's *The Orator.*

(4) Anthony Munday's *Zelauto or the Fountaine of Fame.*

(5) Marlowe's *The Jew of Multa.*

(6) Masuccio's *Il Novellino.*

(7) Gower's *Confessio Amantis.*

(8) *Gesta Romanorum.*

All of these are not of equal importance and there are mainly three which are the significant ones. There is, first of all, a lost old play *The Jew* to which Stephen Gosson refers in his *School of Abuse,* then there is the first work cited by Bullough, the story of *Il Pecorone,* and, third, Bullough's eighth item, the collection of stories, *Gesta Romanorum.* Shakespeare took different parts of his play from these several sources and welded them together to form his own play. Of all these sources, Marlowe's play is the only one still available.

In *Gesta Romanorum* the casket story is a little different. The choice between the caskets is made by a princess, in order to win the Roman Emperor's son for her husband. The inscriptions on the caskets, also, are slightly different:

The Gold Casket—whoso chooseth me shall find what he deserveth.

Silver—whoso chooseth me shall find what his nature desireth.

Lead— whoso chooseth me shall find what God hath disposed to him.[8]

Shakespeare introduces a few minor, but significant changes:

Gold— whoso chooseth me shall gain what many men desire.

Silver—whoso chooseth me shall get as much as he deserves.

Lead— whoso chooseth me must give and hazard all he hath.[9]

Shakespeare, thus, has changed the original story in two ways. The choices are made by men in order to win a lady and the inscription on the lead casket has been made more challenging.

The best contemporary account of the Bond plot is to be found in *Il Pecorone* which is a collection of Italian stories by

Ser Giovanni. The name of the romantic hero is Gianneto and that of the generous friend Ansaldo. Things happen exactly as in the Trial scene in our play. Gianneto's wife comes to the court in disguises and produces the same two arguments as Portia does: no drop of blood must be shed and the Jew must take just one pound of flesh, neither more nor less. It is a matter of special interest to the Indian student that in this connection Bullough refers to the Indian story about how King Ushinara gave his flesh to a hawk:

> The story of the giving of a pound of flesh probably begins in India, for the *Mahabharata* has a tale about King Usinara [...].[10]

The Ring episode is also there in this story, for Gianneto's disguised wife takes his ring. Shakespeare has made it all the more effective by duplicating it with Gratiano and Nerissa. There is a significant change here, brought about by Shakespeare. In *Il Pecorone* Antonio's counterpart Ansaldo is married off to one of the bride's maids (who had helped Gianneto win), but Shakespeare keeps Antonio unmarried.

The Plot of *The Merchant of Venice*

There are four distinct plots in *The Merchant*, as has been pointed out in section (b) of this chapter—the three plots and the Ring episode. Of these, two had already been in existence, but the Lorenzo-Jessica plot and the duplication of the Ring episode are Shakespeare's own. The Bond plot and the Casket plot are both equally important. One cannot call one of them the main plot at the cost of the other. The Lorenzo-Jessica plot is clearly a subplot and the Ring episode is not important enough to be called a subplot—it is an episode or an intrigue. Let us sum up these plots very briefly.

In the Bond plot we see Bassanio requesting Antonio to lend him money which he borrows from Shylock by signing a bond in which it is agreed that, on failure to pay back within three months, a pound of flesh will be given to Shylock from whatever part of Antonio's body he likes. As Antonio fails to pay back, Shylock claims the forfeit. Then Portia saves Antonio by telling Shylock that he (a) must shed no blood and (b) must take just a pound of flesh, neither more nor less. All of Shylock's wealth is taken away as he had plotted against the life of a Venetian citizen. He is given his life on condition that he make Lorenzo his heir and himself turn into a Christian.

In the Casket plot we see Portia, a rich heiress at Belmont, subjected to an extraordinary will left by her father. There are three caskets in one of which Portia's portrait is enclosed. Only the man who can open this casket will be able to a marry her. Several suitors come and two of them try but fail to choose the right casket. Bassanio chooses the right casket and marries her.

In the Lorenzo-Jessica plot we see Lorenzo, a Christian, in love with Jessica, Shylock's daughter and therefore a Jewess. Jessica elopes from home, is converted to Christianity and the two get married. They come to Belmont and eventually Lorenzo becomes Shylock's heir.

In the Ring episode we see Portia and Nerissa, while in disguise craftily taking the rings they had given to their husbands. A quarrel ensues and then Portia reveals the secret of their disguise and how they had saved Antonio.

Shakespeare's genius consists in weaving these separate plots together so as to make a neatly finished whole. Taking the most superficial features first, it can be seen that he has placed the scenes in such a way that the separate plots get the right kind of importance. The scene-wise scheme of location runs like this, with Venice standing for the Bond plot and Belmont for the Casket plot:

Act I —sc. i—Venice, sc. ii—Belmont, sc. iii—Venice.

Act II —sc. i—Belmont, sc. ii, iii, iv, v, vi—Venice, sc. vii —Belmont, sc. viii—Venice, sc. ix—Belmont.

Act III —sc. i—Venice, sc. ii—Belmont, sc. iii—Venice, sc. iv & v—Belmont.

Act IV —sc. i and ii—Venice.

Act V —Entirely in Belmont.

It is easy to see how he alternates between Venice and Belmont, that is, treats the two important plots with equal emphasis. As P.G. Phialas has pointed out:

> In terms of content and location, the scenes of the play are arranged in a way which tends towards close interweaving and unity.[11]

This is the most obvious feature of the plot. There are far more intriguing features, for Shakespeare does not only alternate between the two main plots, he mixes and mingles them till they become almost inseparable. Right at the outset we see that it is because Bassanio wants to go to Belmont that he wants the money from Antonio. From the very beginning, therefore, an intimate link is established between the Bond plot and the Casket plot. As a matter of fact it can be said that the Bond plot depends on the Casket plot for its very existence.

After the bond-signing scene the two plots get separated then in the casket scene, the news about the trial comes and the two plots converge towards each other again. After this in the Trial scene the two merge and in the last Act, consisting of just one scene, all the plots are woven together.

The Lorenzo-Jessica subplot, it is true, is independent of the two main plots, but there are firm links among all three of them. Jessica is Shylock's daughter, so she is a link between the two. The theme of these plots are romantic love, so this and the Casket plot are thematically related.

The Ring episode, also, is related to the Casket plot in two ways. First of all Nerissa is Portia's waiting woman and Gratiano is Bassanio's friend. Secondly, Nerissa in giving and taking the ring copies Portia and this imitation is another link.

Thus, from the very beginning, Shakespeare takes up all the threads of the action and weaves them together with a strong hand so all of them reach a neat conclusion in the last scene. It is the theme of love, moreover, which is common to all. From this point of view it can be said that it is the Casket plot which is the main plot. It is the cause and the Bond plot is the effect.

Thus on the positive side we have the Casket plot and on the other the negative plot of the Bond but both, along with the subplots, are fused into a unified whole. This kind of unity is not to be found in the plays prior to *The Merchant.* It is proof of great command over the art of dramaturgy:

> Here he achieves a cohesion of parts and a unity of the whole which far surpasses what he had attained in his earlier comedies.[12]

Not only has Shakespeare surpassed his earlier plays in the dramaturgy of *The Merchant,* but there are certain other respect in which this play is unique. In all the other plays of this group, that is, *Twelfth Night, Much Ado,* and *As You Like It* the hero and the heroine are betrothed at the very end of the play, sometimes in the very last scene. In this play the hero and heroine of the subplot are not only betrothed but elope and marry in the second Act itself. Then the hero and the heroine of the main plot marry in the third Act, that is, midway through the play. Yet the impression of romantic fulfilment, which should be there at the end of the play, is delayed in a very clever manner. Before Portia and Bassanio can even celebrate, much less enjoy, their marriage, both have to hurry away. So the last scene is the scene of the lover's fulfilment.

There are many different ways in which the plot of *The Merchant* has been explained. A few of them will be given now. The classical viewpoint of Aristotle and his followers treat plot as a separate feature, with but vague links with the theme and the characters. This is not the case now. Instead the plot of a play is related to its theme as well as characters. In a certain case a critic has equated it with a figure of speech.

Taking up the theme of love and of money, C.L. Barber is of the opinion that in this play Shakespeare is showing two different attitudes to money, and the critic then relates this to the plot, for he says that the contrasting attitudes form a pattern in the play:

> [...] the antithetical sort of comic form he was using in this play.[13]

Another extraordinary view is given by Sigurd Burckhardt who considers the plot as the dominant metaphor in the play. This is a complex matter and will be explained in the next chapter. As time goes on, different techniques of criticism emerge and Shakespeare's works are always a constant challenge to all critics. The plot of this play, like its theme and its characters, have been studied from many different points of view.

REFERENCES

1. *The Merchant of Venice,* Act I, sc. iii, ll. 1-3.
2. Act V, sc. i, ll. 286-88.
3. Bradbrook, M.C., *op. cit.*, 88.
4. *Ibid.*
5. Act II, sc. vi, ll. 34-37.
6. Act III, sc. iv, ll. 62-65.
7. Bullough, G., *The Narrative and Dramatic Sources of Shakespeare,* Vol. I. London: Routledge and Kegan Paul, 1957, 445-514.
8. *Ibid.* 514, translated into modern English.
9. Act II, sc. vii, ll. 5-9.
10. Bullough, *op. cit.*, 446.
11. Phialas, P.G., *Shakespeare's Romantic Comedies: The Development of their Form and Meaning.* Chapel Hill: The University of North Carolina Press, 1966, 143.
12. *Ibid.*, 142.
13. Wilders, J., *op. cit.*, 191.

9

IMAGERY AND SYMBOLISM

Shakespeare's poetry is specially rich in imagery and symbolism. It is not certain whether he made use of symbolism with conscious deliberation, but the use of imagery, of course, was deliberate. Sometimes it is difficult to differentiate between an image and a symbol because, most often, images gradually develop into symbols. Let us, however, first have a look at imagery, then the symbolism will be studied.

(a) Imagery

Shakespeare makes use of all kinds of images—sense-images, images drawn from different aspects of nature as well as from different branches of knowledge. There are also copious number of images taken from day-to-day ordinary life, as well as from domestic aspects of life like cooking, sewing etc. Among these, sense images are the most common.

There are five kinds of sense-images, corresponding to the five senses in the human body. Thus images appertaining to the sense of sight are known as visual images, and those to hearing as auditory images. In the same way imagery referring to smell are known as olfactory images, those to taste are gustatory and those to touch as tactile. All such sense-images go to make poetry very rich, for sense-images are far more appealing than, for example, images taken from different branches of knowledge. Again, there are images taken from the world of nature. Images of flowers, trees, birds, rivers etc., appeal to our sense of the beauty and ineffable purity of nature. Imagery from the many different aspects of life give a touch of familiarity to an unfamiliar idea.

Here there is one particular aspect of imagery that has to be kept in mind—often there is overlapping of imagery. That is to say, a nature image will also be a sense-image. If a flower is being described, then it is a nature image, a visual images, and if the fragrance of the flower is mentioned, then an olfactory image as well. If the softness of the petals is mentioned, then, in addition to being a nature image, a visual image and an olfactory image, it comes a tactile image also. Thus, an image can go on becoming more and more complex and the more complex it is, the richer will the poem be.

Sometimes a certain sense-image is described in terms of another sense image. This is known as synaesthesia. Duke Orsino in *Twelfth Night* is talking about music.

> That strain again! It had a dying fall:
> O! it came o'er my ears like the sweet sound
> That breathes upon a bank of violets
> Stealing and giving odour.[1]

Here the duke is describing music with the help of two comparisons (a) sweet sound (b) fragrance of violets. So here auditory and olfactory images have been fused together to describe the music he is hearing. This is a very good example of synaesthesia, uncommon even in Shakespeare.

There are many different kinds of images in *The Merchant.* Apart from sense-images there are nature images, animal images, commercial images and images from the world of art as well. A few of these images can be studied. Since sense-images are the easiest to grasp, they shall be studied first. It should be always remembered that under the category of sense-images, many other kinds of images will automatically come in, since it is through the senses that we perceive the outer world. Thus, naturally, any image will refer to one or the other of our senses. It is very rarely that one can find so abstract an image that it does not refer to any of the senses at all.

Apart from these features, a most important trait about Shakespeare's imagery has been pointed out by Wolfgang Clemen. According to him, in the early part of his career Shakespeare employed imagery in order to decorate his poetry, to highlight the emotion of the speaker or to point out general ideas in a succinct and precise manner. As he developed, however, he made use of less "poetic" and more "dramatic" imagery:

> The more Shakespeare became a conscious dramatic artist, the more he employed them for dramatic purposes.[2]

This is a complex feature, and as the relevant passage comes shall be accordingly pointed out.

From the very beginning of the play, there are passages with great wealth of images. The language of the two young men, Salarino and Solanio, is full of rich images. Thus, right in the beginning Salanio is trying to explain the reasons for Antonio's incomprehensible melancholy:

> Your mind is tossing on the ocean;
> There, where your argosies with portly sail,
> Like signiors and rich burghers on the flood
> Or, as it were, the pageants of the sea,
> Do overpeer the petty traffickers,
> That curt'sy to them, do them reverence,
> As they fly by them with their woven wings.[3]

This passage, from the point of view of imagery, is a very important one, for it displays many interesting features. It will be referred to again and again in the course of this chapter in order to illustrate different features of Shakespeare's imagery. For the present, it should be noticed that the passage contains a visual image in almost every line. In the first line, the mind of Antonio is pictured as tossing like a ship on the sea, then there is the picture of "argosies with portly sail." In the next line, signiors and burghers, richly dressed, are visualized. In the fourth line there is the reference to pageants, that is, to spectacles, with rich visual appeal, then the humbler ships are seen as paying homage to Antonio's ships and finally his own ships are seen as birds.

This particular passage has also been specially selected by Wolfgang Clemen as an example of how Shakespeare uses imagery in order to set the tone of the play:

> As an introduction to the whole play these images are of the greatest importance: they immediately produce the atmosphere of sea, ships and well-to-do merchants in which the play moves.[4]

These images, therefore, are not mere decorations to beautify poetry. They, are, on the contrary, highly functional or, as Clemen says "dramatic," for they serve to create the atmosphere.

This was the first speech of Salarino. In his very next speech we again have a wealth of different kinds of images:

> My wind, cooling my broth,
> Would blow me to an ague, when I thought
> What harm a wind too great might do at sea
> I should not see the sandy hour-glass run,
> But I should think of shallows and of flats.[5]

Here there is a culinary image taken from everyday domestic life ("broth") and the extraordinary image of thc hour-glass. This image is extraordinary because it has been used to suggest something that is most unusual. The hour-glass, normally, denotes the passing of time, but that is not the case here. When Salarino sees the hour-glass he notices the sand in it and this makes him think of sandy shallows against which a ship might knock and founder. Here, therefore, we find an image which has been taken away from its ordinary context, which is the abstract context of time, to focus upon the sand used in it, which is something concrete. Apart from these complexities, there is another dimension to this image. It has been singled out by Clemen as an evidence of how Shakespeare, in his middle period, uses imagery in order to foreshadow later events and also to highlight dramatic irony:

> Here Shakespeare's art of dramatic irony becomes manifest: Salarino, first thinking of his breath with which he cools his soup-imagines what would probably happen if a storm should strike the ships on the high seas.[6]

Salarino imagines what might happen, and what he imagines does really happen, so these images foreshadow coming events. Here again the imagery is not merely decorative, it is highly functional or, in the world of Clemen, "dramatic."

Gratiano's merry sermon against melancholy, among a host of other images, gives three tactile images in as many lines:

> And let my livers rather heat with wine,
> Than my heart cool with mortifying groans.

Why should a man whose blood is warm within
Sit like his grandsire cut in alabaster?[7]

Here there are three anatomical images ("liver," "heart," and "blood") with reference to the sense of touch ("heart," "cool" and "warm"). Then there is an image from the art of sculpture which is also a simile. This entire speech is rich with imagery. A few lines later he gives an auditory image:

As who should say, "I am sir Oracle
And when I open my lips let no dog bark."[8]

These are but a few of the sense-images taken from the first few lines of the play. As has been already indicated, these sense-images also involve other kind of imagery. Ships belong to the category of nautical imagery, so Salanio's ships are visual as well as nautical images. His reference to his physical organs are anatomical as well as tactile, and "mortifying groans" give auditory images. This kind overlapping of sense-images enhance the beauty of poetry.

Examples of synaesthesia also, are not lacking. Thus in Gratiano's speech given above, he is talking of his heart cooling with mortifying groans—both tactile and auditory images are used for the same idea.

Images from nature are scattered throughout the play. One such image is that of tempests at sea, but as this is more of a symbol than an image, it will be necessary to treat it specially, in the next section of this chapter. There are, however, wonderful nature-images besides those of tempests. Salarino gives several images from nature when he talks about possible shipwrecks and rises to a splendid climax:

Enrobe the roaring waters with my silks.[9]

This is a very complex image, for here we have the natural juxtaposed with the artificial—waters and silks, auditory (roaring) along with visual (enrobe) and a metaphor as well, for the roaring waters are imagined as a human being.

In addition, here we have two contrasting ideas which makes the image specially, effective. The stormy seas are contrasted with the smooth and soft silks. This is the effect known as "telescoping of images" as defined by T.S. Eliot:

> Where the most powerful effect is produced by the sudden contrast of associations.[10]

Not only is the natural contrasted here with the artificial, but the rough and destructive sea is contrasted with silks, with associations of softness and richness.

A most effective nature image occurs in Portia's mercy speech. It is an image of only one and half lines, but is so full of rich associations that no more is needed:

> It droppeth as the gentle rain from heaven
> Upon the place beneath.[11]

Here, because of the beneficial aspect of rain, the image is automatically, effective, but in addition, it has religious associations, for God's grace is usually compared with rain.

These are but two of the nature images in the play. There are many more and they are always effective, heightening the beauty of poetry.

Next there are the images taken from different branches of knowledge. There is the famous image from archery used by Bassanio. It can also be designated as a military image for archery is used in sport as well as for fighting. Bassanio uses it with reference to sport:

> In my school-days, when I had lost one shaft
> I shot his fellow of the self-same flight.[12]

This image is elaborated over a few more lines. It is an image from archery and is associated with sport as well as with fighting. It is, in addition, a visual image. A few lines later we have an image drawn from geography:

> Nor is the wide world ignorant of her worth
> For the four winds blow in from every coast
> Renowned suitors.[13]

There are numerous classical allusions in the play. These too can be classified as images taken from classical mythology.

> Her sunny locks
> Hang on her temples like a golden fleece
> Which make her seat of Belmont Colchos' strand
> And many Jasons come in quest of her.[14]

Here the image of Portia's sunny hair is elaborated over four lines with the image of the golden fleece taken from classical literature. Bassanio's language is a language full of images and figures of speech. He takes an image from Roman history to describe Portia:

Nothing undervalued
To Cato's daughter, Brutus's Portia.[15]

Animal images are plentiful in the play. Shylock, for example, is always referred to as a dog, a cur, and in his turn he himself uses animal imagery with references to Launcelot Gobbo:

Snail-slow in profit, and he sleeps by day
More than the wild-cat: drones hive not with me.[16]

Here there are three animal images in two lines. These images all have negative associations, which is not always the case. The image of a bird used by Salarino in connection with Antonio's ships ("As they fly by them with their woven wings") is a positive image. In referring to Shylock, however, everyone uses animal imagery in a negative manner. He himself knows that the Christians call him a dog and he turns the image on them when he has the chance to do so:

Thou call'dst me a dog before thou hadst a cause
But since I am a dog beware my fangs.[17]

The most remarkable animal images are used by Gratiano in the Trial scene when Shylock remains impervious to all pleas of mercy. In this speech there are only animal images. All of them, describing Shylock, are negative images:

O, be thou damned, inexorable dog!
And for thy life let justice be accused.
Thou almost mak'st me waver in my faith
To hold opinion with Pythagoras
That souls of animals infuse themselves
Into the trunks of men: thy currish spirit
Governed a wolf, who hang'd for human slaughter
Even from the gallows did his fell soul fleet
And whilst thou lay'st in thy unhallow'd dam
Infused itself in thee: for thy desires
Are wolfish, bloody, starved and ravenous.[18]

There are no less than four animal images in this one passage. There are two short ones in the first and the last lines each, and a vague one in the reference to Pythagoras. But the elaborate image of the soul of the hanged wolf infusing itself into the as yet unborn Shylock is a long and remarkable image, evoking disgust in the heart of the reader. There are not a great number of such images in Shakespeare, and in this play there is just this one. It is a long image, going on for six lines, entirely negative. It is thought that here he is referring to a contemporary event, when a Jew named Lopes was hanged. It attracted considerable attention and Shakespeare seized the chance.

Not all animal images are so violently negative. Portia also employs animal imagery in a negative manner, but hers are gentle ones. She calls one of her suitors a colt and when the Prince of Arragon fails to choose the right casket she says "Thus hath the candle singed the moth." These are negative images but there is no violence or disgust in them. Her most remarkable use of animal imagery occurs in the last scene, in the context of music:

> The crow doth sing as sweetly as the lark
> When neither is attended, and I think
> The nightingale, if she could sing by day,
> When every goose is cackling would be thought
> No better a musician than the wren.[19]

Here there are five birds mentioned in as many as five lines. The thought expressed may not be one with which a modern reader might agree, but Portia's use of bird-imagery is to be admired. Here there are visual images as well as auditory ones, for the birds can be seen and their song heard. At first, the images are used in a positive manner, for the crow is said to be singing as sweetly as the lark, and then there is a negative image, for the nightingale is not supposed to be singing, in the daytime, at all well. There is also contrast between the crow and the lark, and the nightingale and the goose and the wren.

It has been pointed out that very often Shakespeare is not content with giving just one image. He piles one image on another and the accumulation of images gives a rich and complex effect to Shakespeare's language. In the passage quoted above, there are five bird-images in as many lines.

Here the images are of the same type; that is, all are not only animal images, but about the same kind of animals, that is, birds. Sometimes, however, different types of images follow in quick succession. Thus Antonio refers to the uselessness of asking Shylock for mercy or even consideration.

> You may as well go stand upon the beach
> And bid the main flood bate his usual height
> You may as well use question with the wolf
> Why he hath made the ewe bleat for the lamb
> You may as well forbid the mountain pines
> To wag their high tops and to make no noise.[20]

Here each image takes two lines, and for purposes of emphasis, each image begins with the same phrase "You may as well." This repetition adds to the effect. In addition, though all the three are from nature (the sea, the wolf and the pines) each is taken from a different aspect of nature. Here again, there are visual as well as auditory images—the wolf has made the ewe bleat and the pines are making noise.

Such accumulation of images occur again and again in Shakespeare. In *The Merchant* itself there are many such. There are many other kinds of images to be found by a careful reader.

(b) Symbolism

Symbols go beyond the obvious meaning of the word or the object used, and spread out to give it a wider, deeper significance. Symbolism, therefore, adds to the meaning. Symbols have been classified into different categories by different writers. They have also been defined in many different ways. The definitions given by such poets who have themselves used symbols are of special significance, as, for example, those gives by Yeats and Coleridge. The latter, for example, thinks that a symbol is organically linked with the thing for which it stands. It is no mere substitution. Several different characteristics are also given.

Definitions or classifications of symbols were not available to Shakespeare, for this is a modern development. This, of course, does not mean that such definitions or classifications would be irrelevant to a study of Shakespeare's works. These are but tools which, when applied, enable us to appreciate and understand him better.

The most obvious and important use of symbolism in *The Merchant* are the three caskets. They are very complex symbols and signify many different things at one and the same time. We shall first have a look at some of them. As different critics give their different views it will become clear how complex the symbolism of the caskets is.

It has been said that all the three caskets as well as the Casket scene itself, present the problem of Judgement by Appearances. According to R.C. Moulton this is an everyday problem and Shakespeare has presented an idealized version of it. Shakespeare's artistry lies in glorifying the very common problems of ordinary life and presenting it, in an idealised form, in drama. According to this critic the three inscriptions on the three caskets are such that no amount of reasoning can justify preferring one above the others. There is actually nothing to choose, and it is this fact which shows the problem symbolized by the caskets in an idealized form:

> [...] we, the spectators, can see that from the nature of the problem no reasoning can possibly avail them, we have clearly the problem of Judgement by Appearances drawn out in its ideal form.[21]

The father of psychology, Freud, has given some very valuable interpretations. First of all he quotes another scholar with whom he agrees. According to both of them the Prince of Morocco symbolises the sun, the Prince of Arragon symbolises the moon and Bassanio symbolises the star youth. Freud then interprets the caskets themselves and according to him the caskets are women. They, he declares, are

> Symbols of the essential thing in woman and therefore of a woman herself.[22]

These are two of the early symbolic interpretations of the caskets and their choosers. After this there have been many other interpretations. One reason for this wealth of interpretations is that there are three different things involved here (a) the metals of which the caskets are made, (b) the inscriptions on them, and (c) the contents of the caskets. All these three can be interpreted in different ways and therefore the complications have become so confusing.

Apart from these very clear symbols, there are certain other symbols in this play. Two such symbols are those of "tempest" and "music." It is G. Wilson Knight who has given this interpretation. According to him throughout Shakespeare's work, tempests and music have certain deeply symbolic associations, and in no other play of this period are these better highlighted than in this one:

> In no play of this period is there so close and significant a contrast between the tempest of tragedy and the music of romance.[23]

According to him tempests symbolize strife, loss and tragedy, while music symbolizes harmony and love. He gives, thereafter, a detailed analysis of all the tempests mentioned in the play. There are many such references and they always symbolize loss and violence, as, for example, in the speech by Salarino:

> My wind cooling my broth
> Would blow me to an ague, when I thought
> What harm a wind too great might do at sea.[24]

Not only are there many other references to tempests, but tempests actually figure in a crucial manner. Antonio's ships are lost in tempests. Thus they are not merely symbolic of tragic loss, but they really do bring tragedy to Antonio.

Music symbolizes love and harmony and there are not only references to music, but actual music is present. There are two occasions, both significant ones, when there is music on the stage. One is the Casket sense, where the only song of the play is sung. Then, again, in the last scene instrumental music is played. In this latter scene the symbolic associations of music with harmony is stressed by Lorenzo in two wonderful passages:

> In his motion like an angel sings
> Still quiring to the young-eyed cherubins:
> Such harmony is in immortal souls.[25]

Then, again, he describes the soothing influence of music on human souls and declares that a man who remains unmoved by music is not to be trusted. Thus music stands for the best elements in human nature.

These are the most dominant symbols in the play, but apart from these there are other, lesser symbols as well. The very characters are taken to be symbolic representations of certain feelings and traits. Thus Shylock is taken to symbolize (a) villainy (b) vengefulness (c) greed for gold (d) usury. Portia is taken to symbolize (a) love (b) wealth and, in a highly negative interpretation, (c) the pretentious and hypocritical casket of gold.

Referring to the "fancy" song, Wilson Knight says that this song, besides symbolising love, also serves a symbolic function. It shows in its own way, the thoughts that besiege Bassanio's mind:

> In other words it is symbolic rather than dramatic. A function which Shakespeare's songs very often perform.[26]

The numerous symbols and images in the play thus form an integral part of its effects. They not only make the language rich, but add to the meaning by making it more complex. They add a different depth and dimension to simple description and without them the play would have lost a great deal of its beauty and effectiveness.

REFERENCES

1. *Twelfth Night,* Act I, sc. i. ll. 7-10.
2. Clemen, W., *The Development of Shakespeare's Imagery,* 2nd edn. London: Methuen, 1977, 81.
3. *The Merchant of Venice,* Act I, sc. i, ll. 8-14.
4. Clemen, W., *op. cit.,* 82.
5. Act, I, sc. i, ll. 22-26.
6. Clemen, *op. cit.,* 82.
7. Act, I, sc. i, ll. 85-88.
8. Act, I, sc. i, ll. 97-98.
9. Act, I, sc. i, l. 34.
10. Eliot, T.S., *Selected Prose,* Penguin Books, 1958, 112.
11. Act, IV, sc. i. 189-90.
12. Act, I, sc. i, ll. 140-41.
13. Act I, sc. i, ll. 167-69.
14. Act I, sc. i, ll. 169-72.
15. Act I, sc. i, ll. 165-66.

16. Act II, sc. v, ll. 48-49.
17. Act III, sc. iii, ll. 7-8.
18. Act IV, sc. i, ll. 30-41.
19. Act V, sc. i, ll. 110-14.
20. Act IV, sc. i, ll. 72-77.
21. Wilder, J., *op. cit.*, 43.
22. *Ibid.*, 60.
23. *Ibid.*, 81.
24. Act I, sc. i, ll. 23-25.
25. Act V, sc. i, ll. 67-69.
26. Wilders, J., *op. cit.*, 100.

10

STYLE: DICTION AND VERSIFICATION

The poetic style of any poet has two aspects: (a) the language and (b) the versification. Of these two, diction or language, has been given the third place by Aristotle. As has been pointed out earlier, many of the concepts of Aristotle, though pertinent to tragedy, are relevant for comedy as well, and this is one such case. Both diction and versification, however, go to mark out the individuality of a poet.

There were many theories of diction which were available to Shakespeare, for the Greek and Latin theories of diction were very highly developed. As far as versification is concerned, this aspect of poetry did not receive as much attention as diction did. Horace, for example, with whom the Elizabethans were more familiar than with Aristotle, has a clear-cut theory of diction, but does not pay much attention to versification.

An important aspect of the poetic style of Elizabethan drama should always be remembered: these plays made use of both prose and verse. Normally the main characters who were usually of noble lineage spoke in poetry and the humbler characters in prose. There are, of course, a few exceptions, but this tradition is generally followed by Shakespeare. Sometimes he gives prose even to his major characters, but there is always a valid reason for doing this. From this purely technical point of view, thus, Elizabethan plays differ from the earlier plays as well as from later plays like Restoration comedies. When the Romantic poets imitated the Elizabethan plays, they were careful in observing this convention. The discussion of poetic style, therefore, will have to consider both of these aspects.

(a) Poetic Diction

Some of the most important and basic rules of poetic diction which Shakespeare must have known and followed are: the diction of a character must be in keeping with his age, sex and station in life. This is a very elementary rule. Since in drama it is the individual characters who speak, their speech should be in accordance with their personality. A child should speak differently from an adult or aged person. A female character should be given soften and more polished diction than a man and a servant should not speak as his master does. A villager should not speak as a cultured man of the world does. Portia must not speak as Shylock does—she is a young female character and Shylock is a middle-aged Jew. Launcelot Gobbo must not speak like Shylock or Bassanio, for his social position is that of a servant, though he is a male like them, and perhaps of the same age as Bassanio. The problem of social position is usually solved by giving poetry to the noble characters and prose to the inferior characters. It should be remembered that this is not always the case for in our play Portia herself uses prose as well as verse, and so does Nerissa who is only a waiting-woman. Salarino and Solanio both, though nobly born, are after all minor characters, but they never speak in prose. Yet Shylock, a towering figure, speaks the most effective prose passage in the play, perhaps the most forceful prose passage in the whole of Shakespeare. Two other minor characters who always speak in verse are Lorenzo and Jessica and some of the best poetry in the play has been given to them. Thus, though minor and socially inferior characters speak in prose and the nobly born or the main characters in verse, there are no hard and fast rules in this respect. Much depends upon the individual character itself.

Another rule which has been specially pointed out by Aristotle in the very definition of tragedy itself, is that the diction should be properly embellished in different parts of the play. This too is a rule that should not be limited to tragedy, and is generally held to be true for all kinds of drama. In other words it would mean that the situation in a particular scene will regulate the diction. The same character should not speak in the same manner, for example, when he is chatting with his friends and when he is courting his beloved. Portia should not (and does not) talk in the same way as she does when laughing with Nerissa at the suitors, and in the Trial scene. Here her diction should be (and is) clever and sober, not light-hearted, and Shakespeare, accordingly, gives her the appropriate kind of diction.

It is necessary, moreover, that the diction be properly "embellished" in different ways in different parts of the play. Here the question of rhetoric or figures of speech is concerned. A plain and simple diction is not recommended for drama. The style can be the grand style or middle or low, according to the kind of play it is, but figures of speech are to be used, even in low style. The words used may be elevated or colloquial speech but there is no need for the low style to be entirely without figures of speech. This is seen even in Shylock. His style is very rarely so simple as to be without any figures of speech or images, though it is the simplest in the play.

There are many other rules of poetic diction, given by critics later than Aristotle, but these are the most elementary ones. Horace, for example, recommends the use, though sparingly, of newly-coined words or of words that have dropped out of use. Likewise, there are other poets and critics and dramatists who have their own theory of diction. Shakespeare himself was very fond of word-play (like pun etc.), but never liked bombastic or even pompous language and often parodied them. A master like him always modulates the style to suit the speaker and the situation so that the diction is always realistic, appropriate and yet distinctive. It is a miracle of achievement so that hundreds of his phrases and lines have become household words.

Diction in the *Merchant of Venice*

The diction, used by Shakespeare in this play is fully suited to romantic comedies. It is a rich diction with many figures of speech and is artistically as well as realistically modulated to suit each character. The aristocratic characters (for example Antonio, Bassanio, Portia and a few more) each speak in polished yet unaffected diction, but their language naturally differs from each other's. These differences and varieties have been indicated in a brief but clear manner by P.G. Phialas:

> Shylock speaks a direct, immediate, lucid prose and a staccato verse, innocent of metaphor and his delivery in both prose and verse varies from soothing gentleness to driving, hammer-like violence. Antonio's speech is quite different, less intense, more metaphorical, with a regular, not to say conventional, movement. Bassanio's speech is the most elegant and Gratiano's the most vulgar in the play.[1]

As we study the different elements that go to make the style of this play, these characteristics will become gradually clear. Let us now consider a few of the more important elements.

Stylistic Devices

There are numerous stylistic devices like imagery, symbolism, figures of speech that Shakespeare uses. Metaphors, similes, puns, etc., are the most obvious ones. These rhetorical devices, specially simile and metaphor also overlap into the category of imagery and symbolism and as such, have already been studied in the preceding chapter. Both Salarino and Solanio are elegant young men and they speak in elegant language, full of metaphors and similes. The other characters also speak in language that is highly metaphorical. There is a remarkable use of analogy in one of Bassanio's speeches:

> In my school-days when I had lost a shaft
> I shot his fellow of the self-same flight
> The self-same way with more advised watch
> The other forth, and by adventuring both
> I oft found both.[2]

He is giving this analogy of a youthful sport to urge Antonio to lend some more money to him though Antonio had already lent him some formerly. This analogy is continued for thirteen lines. Such long and elaborate analogies are difficult to compose successfully. This is an extraordinary example, but there are many short analogies to be found in the speeches of Salarino:

> Should I go to church
> And see the holy edifice of stone
> And not bethink me straight of dangerous rocks.[3]

Here Salarino sees the church which is made of stone and by analogy thinks of other stones, that is, "dangerous rocks" at sea which might destroy his ships. There is religious imagery going hand in hand with analogy here.

Dr. Johnson, after writing an entire paragraph on Shakespeare's quibbles, concludes:

> [...] a quibble was to him the fatal Cleopatra for which he lost the world and was content to lose it.[4]

In other words, Shakespeare was very fond of word-play, like pun, malapropism etc. Portia makes frequent use of pun:

> [...] so is the will of a living daughter curbed by the will of a dead father.[5]

Such puns are numerous in Shakespeare. Here the word "will" is used in two senses, (a) the wishes of Portia (b) the last Will and Testament of her father. Usually more meanings are involved.

The best examples of malapropism are to be found in the speeches of Launcelot Gobbo and his father, Old Gobbo:

> Old Gobbo: He hath a great infection, sir, as one would say, to serve [...].
>
> Launcelot: As my father being, I hope, an old man, shall fructify unto you.
>
> Launcelot: In very brief, the suit is impertinent to myself.[6]

Here, in ten lines, are to be found three malapropisms and as the scene proceeds, more come in. Malapropisms are used to provoke laughter, and as Launcelot is a clownish figure, are eminently suited to him.

Word-plays are usual in a clown's speech but here there is a difference between Launcelot and the other clowns or Fools of Shakespeare. The Fools of Shakespeare are a class by themselves. As often as not, they are not really fools for they are quite wise, but as they fill the post of the Court Jester they do the necessary clowning. Yet often, in the guise of foolish sayings, they say wise things. Their speeches are very often full of word-play, but, when they are high-grade clowns, these word-plays are also of a much superior standard than is found here in Launcelot's speeches. Malapropisms, for example, are evidence of ignorance and confusion. Fools like Feste in *Twelfth Night* or the Fool in *King Lear* do not, unless deliberately, indulge in malapropisms. Launcelot is a very low-grade clown, so his malapropisms are evidences of ignorance, not produced deliberately in order to provoke laughter.

Exaggeration or hyperbole is often used in order to heighten the effect or, as in the case of the prince of Morocco, for giving the effect of bombastic boasting:

> I would outstare the sternest eyes that look,
> Out brave the heart most daring on the earth.
> Pluck the young suckling cubs from the she-bear,
> Yea, mock the lion when he roars for prey.[7]

Here the Prince is speaking hyperbolically and, because there are four such hyperbolical images piled on each other, the cumulative effect is one of bombast and not of true valour, which does not boast. It is in this kind of implication that the true mastery over diction lies.

Accumulation is by itself an important stylistic device and Shakespeare uses it again and again in order to intensify the effect. It is not that only the major characters use them, Shakespeare bestows the benefit of his teeming imagination to minor characters too, for, in his very first speech (which has already been analysed for imagery) Salarino says:

> There, where your argosies with portly sail,
> Like signiors and rich burghers on the flood
> Or as it were the pageant of the sea
> Do overpeer the petty traffickers
> That curt'sy to them, do them reverence
> As they fly by them with their woven wings.[8]

Here, in six lines there are, in all, two images ("argosy with portly sail" and "petty traffickers that curt'sy), three similes, (signiors, rich burghers and pageant), one metaphor (fly by them with woven wings). This rich accumulation of embellishments is nothing rare in Shakespeare.

Imagery and symbols also come within the compass of stylistic devices but, as they have been explained in the foregoing chapter, they are not being discussed here. Let us now turn to some devices that are less direct than figures of speech but highly effective components of diction.

Allusion, whether classical or Biblical, is a powerful stylistic device, adding richness and deep overtones to poetry. There are numerous allusions of both of these kinds in this play. One of the first classical allusions occurs when Bassanio describes Portia:

> her sunny locks
> Hang on her temples like a golden fleece
> Which makes her seat of Belmont Colchos' strand
> And many Jasons come in quest of her.[9]

Bassanio is here alluding to one of the best-known classical myths. It is about the hero Jason who went to Colchos to gain the famous Golden Fleece which had miraculous properties. Bassanio's comparison of Portia's golden hair with the Golden Fleece at once turns her into a miraculous, wonderful mythical being and he himself, by analogy, becomes another heroic soul like Jason. Here Shakespeare has used more than three lines for one allusion, but usually the allusions are quite brief. Portia, for example is referring to the conditions imposed upon her by her father's will:

> If I live to be as old as Sibylla, I will die as chaste as Diana.[10]

There are two classical allusions here, in quick succession, in the same sentence.

Biblical allusions, also, are scattered throughout the play. It is mostly in the speeches of Shylock. His allusion to the story of Jacob, the first Biblical allusion of importance in the play, goes on for twenty lines. He, more than anyone else, refers frequently to the Old Testament, but all the allusions are not so long. For example, coming to know about the masquerade that is being planned by the young men, he exclaims:

> But stop my house's ears, I mean my casements:
> Let not the sound of shallow foppery enter
> My sober house. By Jacob's staff I swear.[11]

Not only is there the allusion to Jacob's staff, which is a clear and open allusion, but there is also an allusion which is not so obvious. In comparing the windows of his house with ears he is also obliquely referring to the famous allegory in

Ecclesiastes in which a man's body has been compared with a house. Here it is the opposite—a house is being compared with the human body. Biblical allusions are so natural to him that they are his normal way of thinking, they are not just embellishments.

Irony is a very important feature of style and occurs again and again in *The Merchant.* There are many kinds of irony to be found here. For example it has been pointed out that Bassanio's meditations over gold in the Casket scene are ironical, for though he undervalues gold, yet it is the gold which Antonio has borrowed from Shylock that has enabled him to reach Belmont at all. The entire situation, thus, is ironical. Again, there is dramatic irony in the Trial scene, when Portia and Nerissa are disguised, but no one except the audience knows this fact. When they make their husbands give up the rings and later pretend to be angry, that situation is again ironical, because all the aspects of the episode are not known to the other characters. There are many other such instances of irony. In fact the entire play has been described as an Ironical comedy by Moody. (For more information see the Summing Up.)[4]

Apart from figures of speech, allusions, irony etc., there are many finer points of diction that can be appreciated when particular speeches or scenes are studied. Let us now consider a few such.

Shylock's speeches have received special attention from the point of view of diction. It has been pointed out that his is a comparatively simple style. P.G. Phialas says it is "innocent of metaphor." This is not true, for he makes frequent use of metaphor, as for example in describing Launcelot:

> Snail-slow in profit, and he sleeps by day
> More than the wild cat: drones hive not with me.[12]

Here there are three metaphors in two lines. Shylock is one of those characters in Shakespeare who speak equally well in prose as in verse. In fact his most effective speech is not in verse, but in prose. This speech is one of Shakespeare's most famous prose passages and yet, surprisingly enough, has very few figures of speech:

> I am a Jew. Hath not a Jew eyes? hath not a Jew hands, organs, dimensions, senses affections, passions? fed with same food, hurt with the same weapons, subject to the same diseases, healed by the same means, warmed and cooled by the same winter and summer, as a Christian is? If you prick us, do we not bleed? if you tickle us, do we not laugh? if you poison us, do we not die? and if you wrong us, shall we not revenge?[13]

The speech is much longer, but even these few lines give proof of its power. The diction is so simple as to be conversational speech and it is this simplicity that has made it so effective. Here there are no similes and metaphors to slow down the reader, instead there are rhetorical questions and repetitions that ultimately rise to a crescendo. This simple, unadorned language conveys his searing emotions far more effectively than a host of metaphors could have done.

The romantic moonlit scene of the last Act is in direct contrast to this speech both in mood and in language. Lorenzo and Jessica speak alternately and Shakespeare has created a world of enchantment and romance:

Lorenzo: The moon shines bright.—In such a night as this
When the sweet wind did gently kiss the trees
And they did make no noise, in such a night
Troilus, methinks, mounted the Trojan walls
And sighed his soul towards the Grecian tent
Where Cressida lay that night.

Jessica: In such a night
Did Thisbe fearfully o'ertrip the dew
And saw the lion's shadow ere himself
And ran dismayed away.[14]

The dialogue runs on, with the lovers "out-nighting" each other for several more passages. In all, there are seven such passages. Here we have the figure of speech tautology or repetition, each passage beginning with the phrase "In such a night", and four classical allusions to tragic myths, three of them to tragic love. The entire dialogue starts at and maintains, a high pitch of romantic love, and then, by introducing humour, Shakespeare brings it down to earthly levels. The language remains simple throughout, but the classical allusions give it the necessary dignity.

Portia's mercy speech in the Trial scene is another high spot of the play. Here the language, as befits the theme, is elegant and the movement of the verse is slow. It is one of the most eloquent pieces of persuasive oratory in Shakespeare. It is made all the more effective by the use of religious imagery, beginning with the simile of "the gentle rain" and ending with "It is an attribute of God himself." It is a speech permeated with the basic tenets of Christian theology and it is this, rather than any figures of speech, that makes it so effective. Her argument is both logical and theological:

> That in the course of justice, none of us
> Should see salvation; we do pray for mercy;
> And that same prayer doth teach us all to render
> The deeds of mercy.[15]

It is a very logical argument:

> Justice does not give salvation, but mercy does
> We pray for mercy
> Therefore we should show mercy to other.

It has also been pointed out that there is the evidence of irony in this speech, for when the time comes to show mercy to Shylock, Portia does not practise what she preaches in this speech.

(b) Versification

This is an essential part of poetic style. In fact, diction and versification combine with and supplement each other to make up the poetic style of any writer. No discussion Shakespeare's poetic style is complete without discussing this particular aspect of his poetry. It is a highly technical aspect and only an elementary discussion is possible.

In general, Elizabethan and Jacobean drama was written in a mixture of verse and prose. The verse, again, was mainly blank verse though couplets were used quite often. Blank verse consists of unrhyming iambic pentametre lines and such lines comprise five iambic feet, that is disyllabic feet, of which the first syllable is weak (or unstressed) and the second syllable is strong (or stressed):

He came/too late/the ship/was un/der sail:
But there/the duke/was given/to un/derstand
That in/a gon/dola/were seen/toge/ther
Loren/zo and/his am/orous Je/ssica.[16]

As can be seen, here are four lines of five iambic feet, not rhyming in any way. This is a passage of blank verse.

Versification is a complex matter and there are many features to be noted in it. There are, for example, end-stopped lines and run-on lines. In the passage given above, the first line ends with a colon, that is to say, there is a short pause at the end. When there is this kind of pause, because of a fullstop, comma or any other such punctuation mark, then the line will be called an end-stopped line. On the other hand when there is no such pause then the speaker goes straight on into the next line and the line becomes a run-on line. In the passage quoted above, the first line is an end-stopped line and the next two are run-on ones.

It is an important feature of good blank verse that there are hardly any end-stopped lines in it. If the speaker pauses at the end of each line, then the speech becomes jerky and mechanical. If the character, however, goes on from one line to the next then the verse becomes flexible and natural. It is one of the very obvious reasons for the excellence of Shakespeare's blank verse that his lines, for the most part, are run-on lines.

Sometimes, however, end-stopped lines are deliberately used for specific purposes. Shakespeare deliberately writes end-stopped lines in the famous mercy speech of Portia:

His scepter shows the force of temporal law,
The attributes to awe and majesty,
Wherein doth sit the dread and fear of kings;
But mercy is above this sceptred sway,
It is enthroned in the heart of kings,
It is an attribute of God himself;
And earthly power doth then show likest God's,
When mercy seasons justice. Therefore, Jew
Though justice to thy plea, consider this, [...].[17]

In this passage of nine lines, each line is end-stopped. This is because each line demands attention independently, each line has the force almost of a proverb and should be declaimed in a slow and grave manner. The quality of being end-stopped emphasizes the meaning and the importance of every individual line. What, in the hands of more inferior poets is a defect, has here become a virtue.

Another important feature of blank verse is the position of the medial pause or the caesura. In mediaeval poetry as for example the poetry of Langland, the lines used to be divided into nearly two equal halves and there used to be a pause in the middle of the line. This resulted in very monotonous rhythm. Dramatic blank verse must never be monotonous or mechanical, for here different characters are speaking among themselves, not reciting. So the dramatists, in their blank verse, broke away from the mediaeval tradition and changed the position of the caesura. Instead of putting it right in the middle of the line, they would put it where it seemed to be the most convenient for the actor. Let us look at a few lines of the mercy speech:

> The quality of mercy || is not strained,
> It droppeth || as the gentle rain from heaven
> Upon the place beneath: || it is twice blessed
> It blesseth him that gives, || and him that takes.[18]

The double vertical line marks the position of the caesura, but the actor may change it a little. There is no hard and fast rule—it depends upon the actor. As it is, it can be clearly seen how the caesura changes its position in every line. In the first line it falls after the seventh syllable, in the second after the third, in the third and the fourth lines it comes after the sixth syllable. Thus by varying the position of the caesura Shakespeare has given the speech great flexibility.

It is not necessary for all blank verse lines to be exactly ten syllables in length, because then again there is the chance that the passage may become monotonous. Therefore sometimes there are lines that are slightly longer or shorter than ten syllables, as the case may be. The first passage quoted in this section has got a line that has one extra syllable at the end of the line:

That in/a gon/dola/were seen/togeth/er

This line has five iambic feet and then at the end there is an extra weak syllable. Likewise, there might be a line in which there is an extra syllable in the beginning. In the mercy speech itself there is the possibility of such a line. A clearer example is found in Bassanio's speech:

This is no answer, thou unfeeling man
To/excuse/the curr/ent of/thy cru/elty.[19]

Here the second line has got an extra weak syllable in the beginning. There are such irregularities in poetry, and all such irregular lines have distinct names. The two which have been quoted here are (a) lines wlth extra weak syllable at the end and (b) extra weak syllable in the beginning. They are known, respectively, as Hypermetrical and Anacrutic lines.

Apart from these complexities, it must be remembered that truly good dramatic blank verse is never regular iambic pentametre, for then it would become too monotonous. Therefore the dramatist often introduces other metres, specially trochees and anapaests, to bring about variation in his verse. Look at the third line of the mercy speech:

Upon/the place/beneath/: it is/twice blessed

Here the fourth and the fifth feet are, respectively, a pyrrhic and a spondaic one. This is because the two words "twice blessed" are so important that both should be said with emphasis (so the foot becomes a spondee) and so the two short words immediately preceding it are slurred over so that this foot becomes a pyrrhic.

These are the most important of the purely technical features of dramatic blank verse. There are many other such, like stichomythia, modulation, intonation, etc., that go to create good blank verse.

It now remains to be pointed out that though the major part of the play is in blank verse, yet couplets have also been frequently used. These are special features. Usually at the ends of scenes and Acts the last speech has a couplet at the end, or is itself a couplet. Sometimes a certain moral message has to be imparted, or the situation has to be summed up and this has to be written in such a manner as to receive special attention. Usually the actor (or character) who speaks it comes forward to the part of the stage known as "centre front" and declaims these lines, addressing the audience directly. The best example is the couplet spoken by Gratiano at the end of the play that sums up the mood of the entire play, a humorous, joyous light-hearted mood:

> Well, while I live, I'll fear no other thing
> So sore, as keeping safe Nerissa's ring.

These and other such couplets are in iambic pentametre lines rhyming together and are known as Senecan "sentences" because Seneca's scenes end with such couplets, often pointing out a moral. Shakespeare's couplets, however, do not always point out a moral. The one spoken by Gratiano, for example, is a humorous couplet.

Besides these rhyming couplets, there are a few other passages of rhyming verse in *The Merchant.* The scrolls that the three caskets contain are all in couplets, but in their case both the metre and the length of the lines are different from the Senecan couplets. They are all in trochaic tetrameters. For example the gold casket, opened by the Prince of Morocco has got a scroll saying:

> Áll thăt/glístĕrs/ís nŏt/góld:
>
> Óftĕn/háve yŏu/heárd thăt/tóld:
>
> Mány̆ a/mán hĭs/lífe hăth/sóld
>
> Bút my̆/oútsĭde/tó bĕ/hóld:[20]

Here each line is trochaic tetrametre and two lines rhyme together. There is, however, a little bit of complexity here, for each line lack one weak syllable at the end, that is each line is a catalectic line. Shakespeare has given a colon at the end of each line or a comma to indicate that the reader (or the actor) will have to make a short pause there in order to compensate for the missing syllable. The first foot of the third line is a dactyl and this is because when two metres are mixed, dactyl always goes with trochee and anapaest with iambs.

The art of versification however, is much more complex than these purely technical features can ever hope to explain. Many other features that are not related to prosody also are involved in writing good blank verse. There is also the fact that every poet's verse changes as he progresses in his career. Shakespeare's versification also changes and in *The Merchant* we can see how he has attained mastery over versification.

REFERENCES

1. Phialas, P.G., *op. cit.*, 144.
2. *The Merchant of Venice*, Act I, sc. i, ll. 45-49.
3. Act I, sc. i, ll. 29-31.
4. Brady, F. and Wimsatt, W.K., eds., *Samuel Johnson: Selected Poetry and Prose.* Berkeley: University of California Press, 1975, 309.
5. Act I, sc. ii, ll. 23-25.
6. Act II, sc. i, ll. 120-30.
7. Act II, sc. iii, ll. 28-31.
8. Act I, sc. i, ll. 8-14.
9. Act I, sc. i, ll. 169-72.
10. Act I, sc. ii, ll. 105-06.
11. Act II, sc. v, ll. 34-36.
12. Act II, sc. v, ll. 47-48.
13. Act III, sc. i, ll. 57-65.
14. Act V, sc. i, ll. 1-9.
15. Act IV, sc. i, ll. 203-06.
16. Act II, sc. viii, ll. 6-9.
17. Act IV, sc. i, ll. 189-97.
18. Act IV, sc. i, ll. 183-86.
19. Act IV, sc. i, ll. 63-64.
20. Act II, sc. ix, ll. 65-68.

11
SUMMING UP

We have looked at the different aspects of *The Merchant of Venice* and tried to understand it. Shakespeare's art however, is so complex that the more attentively it is read the more aspects does it reveal. There are many more interpretations of the theme, the structure, the characters, etc., than have been studied here and certain aspects that do not fall within the topics covered up till now will be taken up here.

The Fairy-tale Element/Myth

There is much in this play that sounds like a fairy-tale and the Casket-story is the most obvious of these, though the Bond-story also has the element of fairy-tales in it. Because of this, the entire play has often been designated as a fairy-tale.

The most serious consideration of *The Merchant* as a myth or a fairy-tale is the one given by the father of psychology, Freud. Referring to the three suitors of Portia, he takes the Prince of Morocco as symbolizing the sun, the Arragonian Prince as symbolizing the moon and Bassanio symbolizing the star youth. He says: "our little problem leads us to an astral myth."[1] But this is only one aspect of the Casket story. It does not, according to Freud, truly explain the nature of this intriguing story.

If we study the fairy-tales and myths of different countries then the story of a man or a woman choosing between three objects is found to be a well-known one. Likewise there are stories in which attempts are made by three persons to gain some prize. In every case it is the third person who is the winner or, as it might be, attempts are made three times by the same person and he wins on the third attempt. This is so well-known a feature that "third time lucky" has become a proverb. From this point of view alone it is clear that Bassanio would open the right casket. This is essentially a fairy-tale feature. It also occurs in numerous myths.

The Bond-story is supposed to negate the fairy-tale element. In fact, W.H. Auden is of the opinion that, but for the Bond story, the play is a fairy-tale:

> Omit Antonio and Shylock and the play becomes a romantic fairy-tale like *A Mid-Summer Night's Dream.*[2]

There is, however, the view that the Bond story also has the element of fairy-tale in it. There is the wicked Jew on one hand, plotting against the hero's life, and the angelic Portia on the other, coming to save Antonio. The wicked Jew, like the fairy-tale villain, has no real cause for his villainy. The story requires a villain and so he is there. Against him comes the shining young man who is pre-ordained save him. As Granville-Barker says:

> Then comes this youth [...]. He is life incarnate and destined to victory, and such a victory is the fitting climax to a fairy-tale.[3]

Ironic Comedy

The general opinion about *The Merchant* is that it is a romantic comedy, but a different view is taken by A.D. Moody who considers it to be an Ironic Comedy. There are many other critics who are of the same view. According to this interpretation there are different moral values in the play. The Christian viewpoint is the most apparent one. On one hand the Christian view extols charity, yet it deprives Shylock of everything. Portia who pleads for mercy does not show any mercy to Shylock when the time comes for it. Yet it is the Christians who win in the play. Antonio has repeatedly insulted Shylock and far from repenting it, openly says that he will do so again. Yet he wins in the end and seems to show charity to Shylock by allowing him to live on condition that he make Lorenzo his heir and, moreover, betray his religion. Moody, analyzing the play from this point of view, comes to the conclusion:

> We are subjected disturbingly to two different and unresolved sorts of judgement, two different and unresolved standards of value.[4]

Thus there is a tragic as well as a comic element and the two are kept separate in the play. This becomes apparent in the last scene. Here there is light-hearted rejoicing without any repentance on the part of the Christians at having totally ruined Shylock. The play reflects a highly ironic attitude on the part of the author, which questions the attitude of the audience as well.

Unpleasant Play

Among the many different ways in which *The Merchant* has been labelled, Unpleasant Play is one. First of all, the term "unpleasant play" had been used by Shaw with reference to three of his earliest plays all of which had themes which were highly unpleasant: slum-landlordism, organised prostitution and pseudo-Ibsenite licentiousness. As they castigated these social evils, the plays were highly unpopular. They were, also, severely satirical and the comic element was not very prominent.

In *The Merchant* we have the romantic world of Belmont and the commercial world of Venice, and the two are fully contrasted. The fairy-tale world of Belmont has its own rules, where black is black and white is white and no moral ambiguities are present. It is a world where youthful beauty and love will triumph and everyone will yearn to enter it.

On the other hand there is the realistic world of Venice where the worth of a man is judged by his wealth. Antonio is "good" in Shylock's eyes because he is a wealthy merchant, and for no other reason.

Yet there are ambiguities, Auden declares, and also whether Belmont is really the Earthly Paradise it seems to be, and whether we should, or ought to, want to enter it. Here we find that Bassanio triumphs, yet he is a self-confessed wastrel, a charming fortune-hunter against whom parents caution their daughters in real life. Portia is a daughter, but her conduct in the Trial scene leaves much to be desired. Why does she cause needless mental suffering to Antonio by letting suspense build up till the last moment when she knows that she can put an end to it in a trice? She wants to dramatize herself and gain admiration and praise—not very noble motives.

Moreover, Portia's mercy speech is a piece of eloquent and persuasive oratory, but does she herself show mercy to Shylock? Far from showing mercy, she, as it were, plays with him as a cat plays with a mouse. She promises everything and then takes everything away. After she has ruined him completely, as a man, as a father and as a Jew, there is not even a whisper of regret. Auden declares:

> Watching *The Merchant of Venice* [...] we are compelled to acknowledge that the attraction which we naturally feel towards Belmont is highly questionable [...]. I think *The Merchant of Venice* must be classed among Shakespeare's Unpleasant Plays.[5]

This, however, is slightly different from Shaw's Unpleasant Plays because here the satire on society and its evils is not as prominent as in Shaw. The attitude of moral ambiguity that Auden has pointed out is also not such a clear one as to be universally accepted. On the contrary, the accepted view is that it is a romantic comedy.

Problem Play

This is another label stuck on the play by Auden:

> *The Merchant of Venice* is, among other things, as much a "problem" play as one by Ibsen or by Shaw.[6]

The play, according to him, takes up the problem of usury. This was in important social evil of Elizabethan England and Shakespeare shows that money can be lent both with and without it. There are many critics who have laid emphasis on the theme of usury in this play (see Chapter 5, *supra*). For Shylock however, it is a way of living, however much contemptible it might be.

The Problem Play, as developed by Shaw, has several important features. These plays contain many discussions of the problem which has been taken up, whereas *The Merchant* contains very few such scenes. As a matter of fact, there is hardly any discussion on the problem of usury as such.

Problem Plays, usually, do not merely present a problem, they try to reach a solution as well. No such solution is reached in our play. The individual case of Antonio is solved in a highly individual, not to say unique, manner, but no general solution to the problem of usury has been offered.

Most important of all, in a Problem Play there is never any doubt about the problem which is the central theme of the play. Sometimes there may be more than one problem, but the pride of place is given to that one which is the main theme. It is always in the forefront. The characters, as well as the action, all emphasize it. This does not happen in *The Merchant*. Here the theme of romantic love is extremely important and usury is only a sub-theme. One can at most say that Shakespeare has taken the problem of usury but has not given it the importance necessary for the play to be called a Problem Play. This is a fact recognised by Auden, for he says that *The Merchant* is a Problem Play "among other things." These "other things" then, gain more importance than the theme of usury does.

REFERENCES

1. Wilders, J., *op. cit.*, 60.
2. *Ibid.*, 227.
3. *Ibid.*, 75.
4. Moody, A.D., *op. cit.*, 53.
5. Wilders, J., *op. cit.*, 227.
6. *Ibid.*

12

CRITICAL RECEPTION: A BRIEF HISTORY

The Merchant of Venice, right from its own time, has always been a favourite with all classes of readers. It is prescribed in schools and colleges and is also taken up for research work. This in itself proves the width of its appeal. Comparing Shakespeare favourably with Plautus, Francis Meres mentioned this play among Shakespeare's fine comedies and it was very popular not only with discerning readers but with the ordinary Elizabethan audience. The title-page of the first edition says that it was "diverse times acted by the Lord Chamberlaine his servants"[1] which was the dramatist's own group. The first recorded performance was given at court for King James on Shrove Sunday, 1605 and was so successful that the King ordered another performance on the very next week. It was changed and revised drastically after the Restoration and was performed in that manner till the middle of the eighteenth century.

There were repeated performances in the eighteenth and the nineteenth centuries and the most important feature of the period is the manner in which the character of Shylock was interpreted. It shows how a change in the attitude of the actor as well as the critic had taken place. The actors were very quick to realize the wonderful opportunity the role of Shylock afforded. It had been the custom to present Shylock as a clown and was usually played by comic actors. Then in the eighteenth century he was portrayed as a villain and this became the accustomed way. Then in the beginning of the nineteenth century the star actor Edmund Kean played Shylock sympathetically as recorded by Hazlitt. In the Victorian times

Shylock became a dignified as well as a pathetic figure, a tragic hero. This change in the interpretation of his character reflects the change in the social as well as the critical attitude.

Literary criticism too has been uniformly favourable as well as exploratory, praising the play for its many virtues. N. Rowe, in early eighteenth century, was the first to point to its tragic qualities, mainly because of Shylock but the attitude underwent a drastic change in the next century. The Romantic critics looked upon Shylock as a victim. Hazlitt declares:

> The desire of revenge is almost inseparable from the sense of wrong and we can hardly help sympathising with the proud spirit.[2]

Hazlitt, however, does not write only about Shylock, he gives a systematic full-length appreciation of the play, discussing the craftsmanship, characterization, style, etc.

Heine, the German poet, took a very negative view of each character. Antonio is "a weak creature without energy," Bassanio "a real fortune-hunter," Lorenzo the "accomplice of a most infamous theft." The only character he praised was Shylock.

The idea of a central theme holding the play together was first given by Hermann Ulrici, a German critic of mid-nineteenth century and at the end of the nineteenth century we find a long, serious and systematic analysis of every aspect of the play by R.C. Moulton. The Casket-plot, according to him, takes up the problem of Judgement by Appearance (see Chapter 5, *supra*, for a detailed account).

After this, in the twentieth century there is such a great wealth of critical studies that it is difficult to keep track of them, specially after the Second World War. There are studies of individual characters like Shylock (E.E. Stoll's essay is named after him), of individual features like imagery (as in the books by Caroline Spurgeon and Wolfgang Clemen), painstaking work about the sources (like the work of G. Bullough). Moreover, there are different methods of criticism. There is imaginative interpretation by G. Wilson Knight who emphasizes the recurrence of certain key ideas like those of tempests and of music (see Chapter 10, *supra*).

Critics have also considered the genre of the play from different points of view, looking upon it as a romantic comedy, or otherwise. H.B. Charlton, for example, takes a very sympathetic view of Shylock and also declares the play as not to be considered as a romantic comedy:

> *The Merchant of Venice*, then, is hard to fit into a progressive series of Shakespeare's comedies.[3]

Harley Granville-Barker looks upon it as a fairy-tale and observes that both the Bond story as well as the casket story have elements of the fairy-tale in them:

> There is no more realism in Shylock's bond and the Lord of Belmont's will than in Jack and the Beanstalk.[4]

There is also the view, as far as the genre of the play is concerned, that *The Merchant* is an ironic comedy. This is the view of A.D. Moody (discussed in Chapter 12). W.H. Auden considers it to be an Unpleasant Play as well as a Problem Comedy in the manner of Ibsen and Shaw (also discussed in Chapter 12).

A very important development in modern criticism is the great variety of critical schools based on different branches of knowledge. There are the Marxist and the Psychological schools of criticism in the beginning of the twentieth century. Then, as the decades passed, numerous other such schools developed, like Structuralism, Feminism, Post-Colonialism, Reception theory etc. All these different schools have their own critical methods and terminology. Many of them have interpreted the play accordingly. Freud's essay is one of the earliest interpretations. It explores the mythical and the fairy-tale elements. Both anthropology and psychology are used in this interpretation (vide Chapter 12, *supra*).

Even more recently, in India, there have been attempts at interpreting Shakespeare from the point of view of Indian poetics. There are several schools of Indian poetics, like *Rasavāda, Alaṇkara* and *Dhvanivāda,* which are the most important. A very brief and superficial analysis of the play from the Indian point of view will now be given.

Indian Dramaturgy

According to Indian dramaturgy there are ten kinds of plays (*rūpakas*). This classification has been made with the content, characters and the *angīrasa* in view:

Vastu, netā, rasasteṣāṅ bhedako vastu ca tridhā.[5]

In other words the subject-matter, the hero and the *rasa*—the differences in these three give rise to the difference among the *rūpakas* or plays.

According to this division *The Merchant* will be a *nātikā*, for the story, though well-known, is not as well-known as a myth or a Biblical story. It is not *prakhyāta* but *utpādya*. As a matter of fact, Shakespeare makes several changes even in the stories he uses. The hero, Bassanio is also not a *prakhyāta* hero like one from the epics or a historical figure, he too is *utpādya*. The main or the *angi rasa* is *śṛṅgāra* or the Erotic *rasa*. This is because in spite of many different critical opinions it is generally accepted that it is a romantic comedy, with love as the main theme. *Śṛṅgāra rasa*, as used in the play, fulfils the three conditions necessary for the *aṅgī rasa*, like *vahuvyāpti* etc.

The plot of the play is divided into two main sections. The main plot is known as *adhikārika* and the related stories are *prāsaṅgika*. The *prāsaṅgika* in its turn is divided into two kinds: *patākā* and *prakarī*. Our play presents some problems for here the Portia-Bassanio plot, with *śṛṅgāra* as its main *rasa* should be called the *adhikārika*. The Bond-story, from this purely technical point of view, will have to be called a *patākā*, for it is the plot that continues till almost the end. For Western critics also, the play presents the same problem: which is the main plot of the play, for the two have equal importance? From a technical point of view, the Bond-story will have to be given a minor status since it is the result of the main romantic plot, which is the cause. The Lorenzo-Jessica plot and the Gratiano-Nerissa plot are both *prakarīs*.

The progress of the play has been meticulously divided into many different and complex stages. A full and detailed analysis, which is not necessary here, will make these stages clear. Almost every stage given in Sanskrit theory can be paralleled. Bassanio's asking Antonio for money is the *bīja.*

As far as the characters go, both Antonio and Bassanio are of equal importance. The play is named after Antonio, so let us take him first. According to Sanskrit classification, Antonio will be a *dhīrodātta* character. Such heroes are:

> *Mahāsattva-atigambhīrah kṣmāvānavikatthanah*
> *Sthiro nigurḥāṅkāro dhīrodātta dṛhavrata.*[6]

In other words, the *dhīrodātta* hero has a noble soul, grave demeanour, a forgiving nature, does not brag, is quiet, modest and resolute. Each one of these adjectives fit Antonio. Shakespeare could not have produced a better example of such a hero if he had Ācārya Dhananjaya's definition in front of him.

On the other hand, Bassanio is the typical *dhīralalita* hero:

> *Niścinto dhīralalitah kalāsaktah sukhī mṛduh.*[7]

That is, the *dhīralalita* hero is of carefree nature, loves the fine arts, comfort-loving and gentle in manner. Again, this description fits Bassanio, except for the love of fine arts.

Shylock is definitely a strong *pratināyaka.* Such a character is defined by Ācārya Dhananjaya thus:

> *Lubdho dhīroddhatah stabdhah pāpakṛdvyasanī ripuh.*[8]

He is greedy *dhroddhata,* quiet, sinful, sensual and the hero's enemy. Each of these epithets, again, fits Shylock. Yet Shylock is far more than a mere villain, for Shakespeare's treatment of him generates sympathy and guilt in our minds.

When we come to the female characters, there are many kinds of them in Sanskrit dramaturgy, and they have many attributes. It is difficult to classify Shakespeare's heroines, but Portia can be said to fall within the category of *Madhyā-adhīrā nāyikā: dhīrā sotprāsavakroktyā.*[9] Such a heroine chides her beloved with laughter and irony, indeed, as Portia does:

> Even so void is your false heart of truth
> By heaven, I will ne'er come near your bed
> Until I see the ring.[10]

There are many interesting aspects of Indian theories which help to throw light on many features of Shakespearean comedies.

REFERENCES

1. Wilders, J., *op. cit.*, 13.
2. *Ibid.*, 27.
3. Charlton, H.B., *op. cit.*, 126.
4. Granville-Barker, H., *op. cit.*, 67.
5. Dwivedi, Hazari Prasad, and Dwivedi, Prithvinatha, *Nīṭyaśāstra Ki Paramparā aur Daśarūpaka.* New Delhi: Rajkamal Prakashan, 1971, 67.
6. *Ibid.*, 114.
7. *Ibid.*, 113.
8. *Ibid.*, 122.
9. *Ibid.*, 127.
10. *The Merchant of Venice*, Act V, sc. i, ll. 189-91.

13
IMPORTANT QUESTIONS

(a) Detailed Questions

1. "Shylock is a good hater: a man no less sinned against than sinning." Do you agree? Give reasons for your answer.
2. "Bassanio must not be judged by critical methods which are fair when applied to Romeo." Discuss.
3. "Antonio is drawn as a complete contrast to Shylock in their respective roles of the man of business." Elucidate, with special reference to the text.
4. "Shylock is only defeated by a legal quibble which would be a disgrace to any court of justice." Discuss.
5. "The act of assuming male attire is essentially unwomanly and is bound to lessen the appeal of female character of drama, such as Portia, resorting to it." Comment.
6. "Shakespeare has no poetic justice in his plays, neither does he preach morality. He gives life as he sees it and leaves us to draw our own conclusion." Amplify.
7. "*The Merchant of Venice* loses its appeal because Bassanio is not great enough to be a satisfactory hero." Do you agree?
8. "Shylock is the greatest character in the play." Discuss.
9. "*The Merchant of Venice* does not show that Shakespeare agreed with the injustice shown to the Jews." Elucidate.
10. "A strong but immoral character excels a virtuous

weakling." Compare and contrast Antonio and Shylock in the light of this remark.

11. Comment on the use of prose and verse in *The Merchant of Venice.*
12. Consider *The Merchant of Venice* as a romantic comedy.
13. Consider *The Merchant of Venice* as an ironic comedy.
14. Comment on the element of myth and fairy-tale in *The Merchant of Venice.*
15. What is the central theme of *The Merchant of Venice?* Discuss with special reference to the text.
16. Examine the dramatic structure of *The Merchant of Venice.*
17. Write a note on the imagery of *The Merchant of Venice.*
18. Do the subplots have any relevance in the play? Give a reasoned answer.
19. What are the main sources for the play and how has Shakespeare used them?
20. Write a note on Shakespeare's poetic style in *The Merchant of Venice,* with illustrations from the text.

(b) Short Contextual Questions

1. Explain how Portia's choice of a husband was limited by her father.
2. What were the terms and conditions of Antonio's bond with Shylock?
3. What was the legal quibble with which Portia saved Antonio?
4. Describe the Ring episode.
5. How does Shylock behave on Jessica's elopement? How is it described?
6. Who were the first two suitors and how did they choose the casket?

7. What were the inscriptions on, and the contents of, the caskets?
8. With which nights do Lorenzo and Jessica compare the moonlit night?
9. What steps does Portia take to save Antonio?
10. How does Antonio react when saved from danger and given Shylock's property? What are the conditions he imposes on Shylock?

A SELECT BIBLIOGRAPHY

Bradbrook, M.C. *The Growth and Structure of Elizabethan Comedies.* London: Chatto and Windus, 1955.

—— *Elizabethan Stage Conditions.* Cambr. Univ. Press, 1968.

Brown, J.R. *Shakespeare and His Comedies.* London: Methuen, 1957.

Bullough, G. *The Narrative and Dramatic Sources of Shakespeare,* Vol. I. London: Routledge and Kegan Paul, 1957.

Champion, L.S. *The Evolution of Shakespeare's Comedies.* Harvard Univ. Press, 1973.

Charlton, H.B. *Shakespeare's Comedies.* London: Methuen, 1977.

Clemen, W. *The Development of Shakespeare's Imagery.* London: Methuen, 1977.

Knight, G.W. *The Shakespearean Tempest.* London: Methuen, 1953.

Moody, A.D. *Shakespeare: The Merchant of Venice.* London: Edward Arnold Pubs., 1964.

Ribner, I. *William Shakespeare: Life, Times and Theatre.* New Delhi: Wiley Eastern Ltd., 1978.

Tillyard, E.M.W. *The Elizabethan World Picture.* New York: Vintage, Books. No date.

Wilders, J. ed. *The Merchant of Venice: A Casebook.* London: Macmillan, 1969.

INDEX